WHAT DO YOUR
CUSTOMERS
REALLY WANT?

*Here's a sure-fire
way to find out*

JOHN F. LYTLE

PROBUS PUBLISHING COMPANY
Chicago, Illinois
Cambridge, England

ISBN 1-55738-456-8

Printed in the United States of America

BB

1   2   3   4   5   6   7   8   9   0

To Garri Budunsky, an artist and friend whose discerning eye and intellect inspires my pursuit of true art in marketing

Contents

Preface

This book has its genesis in a proprietary information system called EMS/PerformancePlus. As President of Elmhurst Service Inc., (EMS) a marketing consulting firm, I created PerformancePlus in the early '80s in response to a growing demand for "below-the-surface" customer information. Everywhere I looked (and that included my clients), I saw managers frustrated with superficial customer data. Despite all the advances in market research technology and sophisticated database marketing, companies knew very little about what their customers really wanted.

It wasn't that there was anything inherently wrong with knowing that 23% of your customers located in a given geographical area preferred your product over competitors' products; or that 45% of your potential market answered that they had seen your advertising in the past year and responded favorably to it. But the R&D manager trying to figure out how to allocate his precious resources or the marketing guy trying to take share in the face of increasing competition didn't care much about such statistics. They desired to know what type of products their customers would pay a premium price for or what added product or service feature would bring competitors' customers to their brand in droves.

After much trial and error, I brought PerformancePlus into the market. Though I'll explain its methodology later in the book, for now you should know that it's a tool for unearthing what the customer really wants.

Through a series of open-ended questions and probes employed by skilled interviewers, and through an analysis that puts the responses in quantifiable, highly usable form, we gave our clients an "interior" view of their customers.

We helped them identify not only current customers' needs, but ones that were just starting to emerge, so our clients could be there waiting with exactly the right products and services.

We enabled clients to prioritize customer needs, ranking them in order in seven basic categories and spotlighting what we termed the "superior need."

We offered strategic action plans that suggested logical tactics to capitalize on emerging and superior needs.

Now it is approximately ten years and 12,000 PerformancePlus interviews later. We've conducted those interviews not only in the United States, but in 34 foreign countries. Our clients have been (and are) 100 of the country's leading corporations. As a result of their capitalizing on the information and analysis we brought them, they've gone from market challengers to market leaders; they've introduced highly successful new products and services; and they've greatly improved long-term customer relationships.

Based on what's happened in the past ten years and the 12,000 interviews, I've written this book.

It's not a market research book, at least in the traditional sense of the term. You will find relatively little jargon and few market research perspectives in these pages. Instead, I view market research as a strategic tool, as a way to reveal the most precious secrets customers possess. My premise is: *the more you know what the customer truly needs, the more successful your business will be.* How to find and use that knowledge is what this book is all about.

If you're a general manager, it will assist you in deploying your resources to world class standards of operating achievement.

If you're a product manager, it will give you ideas and approaches to outsell competitors in your category.

If you're a marketing executive, it will provide you with tools that will enhance your advertising's effectiveness.

If you're a product design manager, it will enable you to create a product ideally suited to your customer's specifications.

No matter who you are or where you work, this book offers you methods to gain crucial information—information that will make you that much more effective in your job.

In the following pages, you'll find many examples of companies that have been extraordinarily effective—as well as those that have been ineffective—in their approach to customer satisfaction. Some of the examples involve well-known companies with whom I have no formal affiliation. Others focus on organizations, both named and unnamed, who are or have been clients of my consulting firm. These companies represent a gamut of businesses, both service and manufacturing, industrial and consumer.

I will try to use each example to illustrate a truth about customers that transcends natural boundaries. I've found that the moral of a story about a manufacturer of industrial solvents can be relevant to a manufacturer of children's toys. Though the environments are different, the process of meeting customer needs remains the same.

You'll also note that the beginning of each of the seven "customer need" chapters contains a short quote. These quotes are excerpted from "verbatims"—interviews we conducted on behalf of clients with various customer groups. I've included these quotes to let you eavesdrop on the customer voice, to give you a sense of what customers sound like when they reveal truths about what they like and dislike, what they need and don't need.

If you listen to the customer voice long enough and hard enough—and if you ask the right questions and analyze the responses properly—something magical happens. You come upon a piece of information that is so significant, it can transform your business. It's the nugget that every organization always sifts for but rarely finds, the one that leads to a vein of gold.

I call that nugget the superior customer need, and this book will show you how to find it and to mine it for all that it's worth.

Acknowledgment

There have been many special people who have touched my life, each leaving a residue of value that has become the well-spring of my heart.

My wife Mimi and I are pleased to share with you our decision to donate all profits, after taxes, from the sale of this book to educational and charitable purposes. We encourage you to give of your time, talent and treasure to address the needs you encounter within your own communities.

It is my hope and dream that the world can be a safer, friendlier place for our children and our children's children.

God bless you.

John Lytle

Chapter 1

A Working Definition

I f you want to find out what your customers really want, you have to discover what they really need. As you've certainly learned over the years, customers need many things. Or they say they need one thing, but really want another. Or they miscommunicate or you misinterpret their priority of needs.

Whether your customer is an end user or a purchasing agent, he has one need that towers over all others. You may not know what that need is, even your customer may be unaware of it. But it exists in various forms and guises. I call it the "superior need," and if you meet it, you've met the toughest test of customer satisfaction.

A customer can have more than one superior need. I realize that's a contradiction from a grammatical standpoint, but from a customer satisfaction standpoint it makes sense. When I refer to a superior need, I'm talking about a need in each of the following seven categories:

♦ Delivery

♦ Customer service

♦ Company image

♦ Emergencies

♦ Product quality

♦ Pricing

♦ Research and Development

This superior need does more than simply satisfy the customer; it delights him. Therefore, it goes beyond the usual customer satisfaction standards—they don't even have a measurement on their scale for delight.

I'm going to show you how to reach "delight." The process begins with an understanding of different levels of customer satisfaction, and how they connect to superior needs.

ANTICIPATING NEEDS

The typical way of looking at customer satisfaction involves past and present customer relationships (see Figure 1.1). If you want to meet a superior customer need, you look to present and future relationships.

For instance, you're a company that supplies pumps to a papermill. One day, you learn that the papermill has changed its manufacturing process. In short, they no longer need pumps.

From a customer satisfaction perspective, you've done all the right things. Your pumps met all the specs, and for 25 years, the customer has been satisfied with your product.

Figure 1.1   **Dramatically Different Attitudes Exist1**

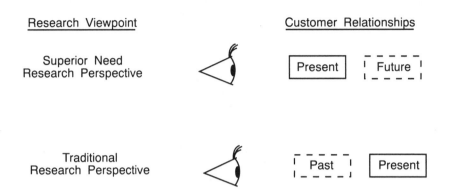

Research Viewpoint   Customer Relationships

Superior Need
Research Perspective   Present | Future |

Traditional
Research Perspective | Past | Present

While a traditional research perspective causes you to react to marketplace needs and expectations, a superior need research orientation causes you to be proactive and capitalize on emerging opportunities.

What have you done wrong? You've failed to anticipate your customer's emerging needs; you've failed to acknowledge that what satisfies them today may not satisfy them tomorrow.

How many companies not only anticipate customer needs, but provide a product or service based on that anticipation? Not many. Not many can take the mandated "leap of imagination."

Interplak did. They went into a market where customers paid between $1 and $3 for a toothbrush and charged $79 for their Interplak system. They anticipated their customers' need for a toothbrush that removed plaque and tartar and created a brushing system that met the need. Therefore, they did more than meet a present need or conform to past standards.

They created something new, based on where the market was going. Interplak wasn't deterred by customer satisfaction; namely, price. They looked at price from a superior need perspective. They said the following:

♦ Our customers are spending around $70 for two visits to the dentist each year to have their teeth cleaned.

♦ They're spending hundreds of dollars more on cavities caused by plaque and tartar.

♦ They're spending time away from their jobs because of visits to the dentist.

Interplak concluded that $79 was not too great a price to pay for the satisfaction that its product delivered.

CUSTOMER PERSPECTIVES

Today, most companies provide their customers with a range of services, and those services offer "value" to customers. But how many companies take their services to the next value level? Neither values nor customer needs are static; they migrate upward and away at a furious pace. I call this difference between your current performance and their requirements the expectation gap (see Figure 1.2). If you don't anticipate and market toward that migration, you'll be left in the dust. Nowhere is this migration of values and needs more evident than in the diaper industry. Not so long ago, cloth diapers were the standard. Then, in rapid succession, new and improved features were added in response to customer needs, including disposable plastic diapers, inner liners to prevent rashes, deodorizers, contoured shape and resuable tape that didn't tear the diaper, increased absorption—the list goes on and on. Players in the industry had to keep moving quickly to new and improved value levels or they would be out of business.

Companies that are able to move to these higher levels provide hyper-service, and they increase the odds of meeting the superior need.

Hyper-service means going beyond the basics. It means offering customers better-than-average quality, very competitive prices, and delivery that's faster than others. It means designing an additional menu of services that competitors don't offer. It could involve

Figure 1.2   **Expectation Gap**

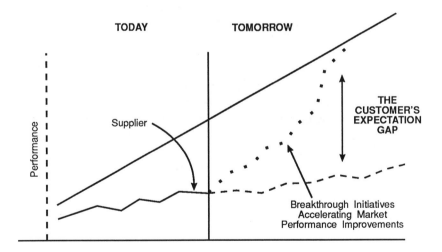

fix-it service on demand (in-home or in-plant), emergency resources, and so forth.

Above hyper-service, there's another level called "partnership fervor." Rather than taking the typical stance of "I've got a product, you want to buy it?" partnership fervor implies a pact between supplier and manufacturer, company and consumer. It requires you to explore with your customer where he's heading and to help him get there. The pact demands that you provide product and service support for both the short- and long-term commitments. It's support that changes as the customer's needs change.

For example, let's go back to our toothbrush for a moment. You're a supplier of plastic fibers used in manual toothbrushes. One of your customers comes to you and explains that they're developing a new electronic brush that will require fibers that can withstand a rotational force of 1,200 cycles per second. You sign a nondisclosure agreement with your customer, and they show you what they're working on.

What do you do next? Are you willing to commit the resources to develop a fiber that will meet the customer's needs? Is it really worth it, since there's no guarantee your customer's product will ever reach the marketplace or sell even if it does? After all, there are a lot of companies making manual toothbrushes; why not be content with that market? Well, because you'll miss the chance to satisfy a customer's superior need; that is, a chance to give him what he really wants.

To satisfy a customer's future needs is difficult. To drum up the partnership fervor necessary to meet those needs is even more difficult. But it's worth it, both for you and your customer.

WHY COMPANIES DON'T KNOW
WHAT THEIR CUSTOMERS WANT

Two-thirds of this country's companies fail to satisfy superior needs because their perceptions of what their customers really want are far from reality.

It is not because they don't care about the customer's needs; other facts are needed. For about one-third of this group, the problem is arrogance. It's the paternalistic attitude that "I know what's best for my customers." Then, the answer is: How do they know what's best?

"Because I talk to my customers every day," they explain. "Because I have thousands of people in my sales force, in my customer service department, and in my research and development group. They tell me what's going on."

They fail to understand that the superior need is rarely discerned within the highly-charged atmosphere of a sales or service call. How can it be when the sales or service person is focusing on matters at hand, such as making a sale or solving a problem?

Companies with this attitude rarely, if ever, conduct research. They rely on information filtered through a thousand voices, a thousand biases, and a thousand personal agendas. Though their intentions are honorable, the result is information that is woefully distorted.

Another one-third of the group conducts research the old-fashioned way. Typically, they attend a trade association meeting and hear that a number of competitors have hired big research firms to survey their customers on a particular subject. Frequently, they latch on to a particular question that's part of the survey. When they return from the meeting, they call in a subordinate and say, "I want you to find the answer to this question. Get a market research firm to conduct a study."

The subordinate follows instructions. He finds a firm that will send a closed-end (yes-no answers required) survey to thousands of people. The survey comes back with unambiguous, easy-to-understand information: 40% of those surveyed believe your product is priced too high; 75% prefer Brand X over your product because it has Feature A.

All the questions are answered, and decisions can be made based on those answers. The only problem, of course, is that such answers are flawed. They're incomplete, surface responses that don't approach the real issues. They are nothing more than statistics, lacking the depth open-ended research can provide (see Figure 1.3).

The remaining one-third use both closed-ended and open-ended research to delve into the real challenges and opportunities their customers face. As you'll see, they not only ask the right questions, but they also ask them in the right way.

THE DANGER OF FALSE RESEARCH

Not long ago, our office had a serious problem with our telephone system. I called my sales representative at the phone company, and the woman who answered said my rep wasn't there. I asked for her back-up, and was told that she wasn't sure who it was. We left it that either the rep backing up her accounts or the shift supervisor would call me back. Five days passed without anything happening. Finally, and ironically, my rep returned from a customer service training workshop. She returned my call and got someone to come out to fix the problem.

Figure 1.3	**Research Modalities**

Closed Ended Approach

Statement: I believe quality to be evidenced by the outward appearance of a product.

(Please indicate the response below which most accurately reflects your attitude towards the above statement.)

Strongly Disagree	Somewhat Disagree	Neutral	Somewhat Agree	Strongly Agree
☐	☐	☐	☐	☐

This captures statistics.

Open Ended Approach

Question: What are the elements that comprise your definition of quality?

Initial response: _____

_____

_____

1st Probe: Has your definition changed in the last two years?

Response to 1st probe: _____

_____

_____

2nd Probe: In what ways do you see your definition changing in the next two years? And why?

Response to 2nd probe: _____

_____

_____

This captures the true voice of the customer - in his own vocabulary.

A little while later, I received a call from a research firm hired by the phone company to survey customer opinion of the company's technical service. The researcher asked, "How would you characterize your satisfaction with the service you received?"

I described the process that I went through, ending by saying that the system was fixed when someone finally came out to our company.

As soon as I finished my rather lengthy answer, the researcher asked another question. I knew that it was impossible for anyone to write down even half of what I said without more time. So I asked the researcher what he had written for my response.

"Satisfied," he replied.

I said I didn't understand how he could write that answer, given what I had told him.

"Look," he said. "There are only two responses: satisfied and not satisfied. They fixed your system, so you're satisfied, right?"

Wrong. In fact, I'm in the market for a system upgrade, and I'm going to purchase it from one of my phone company's competitors.

What's the point of this type of research? hen they're done, the phone company will receive results indicating that a majority of their customers are satisfied. Perhaps it is some lower-level type of customer satisfaction. But it is not the superior need type.

When I read in the papers that the telephone company is downsizing 22,000 employees, I'll know where part of the problem lies.

If my phone company really wanted to determine if its customers were satisfied, they might have taken the following approach:

"Mr. Lytle, I'm calling on behalf of _____. They're making a serious effort to determine your satisfaction with your technical service requirement. Can you tell me, in a nutshell, the circumstances surrounding the situation that occurred last month?

"Now, when you first contacted us, what happened? Where did it lead to? Were you satisfied when the problem was finally fixed? Was your loss of time because of the phone problem costly? What instructions that you gave to us weren't followed up, and how did you feel about that? If you could tell management one thing about how to enhance their ability to serve people like you, what would it be?"

They wouldn't have to ask thousands of customers these questions—100 or so would suffice. The responses would provide a pattern indicating that the people in the technical support group aren't well-trained, and that they view their jobs as taking phone inquiries and writing messages on memo pads.

If management acted on that information and improved training, they would invariably increase customer satisfaction and customer retention levels.

COMBINING RESEARCH METHODS

The combination of closed-ended and open-ended research is synergistic. Consider the following scenario. A major power tool manufacturing company commissions a direct mail survey asking: Do you believe that a quality product is defined by durability, yes or no?

About 27% of those who respond say no, the rest say yes. If you stop here, you'd probably think that it's accurate to assume that durability equals quality; that the 27% who disagree are the type of people who enjoy being contrary. The majority wins.

But what if you conduct open-ended research with the 27% who disagree?

One of the disagreers, a design engineer at a large plant, might say, "For a cheaper drill, you might not want one that lasts for 6,000 hours. For an expensive drill, 6,000 hours might not be enough. So when you ask, is durability the same as quality, I'd answer, it all depends on the context of what."

"The context of what" is the key. Some people disagree because quality is based on a particular set of circumstances. Opened-ended research can pinpoint those circumstances.

For instance, we might ask our design engineer, "What are the elements of quality as it relates to what you're doing?"

"Well," he'd respond, "we've invested a lot of money in creating quality specs, and we need to know our suppliers meet or exceed every one of those specs."

Once a researcher hears those words, he might think: "Meet or exceed specs is what defines quality" and stop there. But you have to continue to probe. For instance: "What are main components of your specs?"

Such a question might cause the engineer to discuss the three different types that concern his company: military, ASTM standards, and European standards.

Then the researcher can ask, "How do you measure quality? Is it a formal or informal process?"

The design engineer says, "In the past, if we got a part back, we threw it in a bucket, and when the bucket filled up, we knew we had a problem. Very informal, but we've changed. Now, we need to know coming off the dock that a part is defect-free. We don't have a quality control department, so it's up to our vendors to give us a certificate of full quality control inspection."

There are other questions, but I think you see my point. You can't be content with the easy answer. You have to dig for information that will provide a way for you to become strategicially or tactically different by adding value to a product or service.

In short, you can't just ask people if they feel bad today. If you do, all you'll learn is that 27% of the people surveyed feel bad. You need to discover why they feel bad and what it would take to make them feel better.

If you only have a vague understanding of why your customer is dissatisfied, you can only provide vague solutions. Sometimes, what your customer really wants is complicated. Sometimes, he has to talk about his problmes for a while before he realizes his biggest need.

TRANSLATING RESEARCH INTO TACTICS

When a credit card company asked my firm to determine how people defined quality in a credit card, 62% of respondents answered: American Express.

We took it a step further: we asked those 62% for the three things they liked best about American Express. They responded with a list of numerous features.

Then we asked the 38% who didn't respond with American Express specific questions to determine how they defined quality in a credit card. The majority talked about clear, understandable documentation for transactions; many complained about the lack of this documentation in their credit cards.

Voila! Our client (who, needless to say, wasn't American Express) had a possible tactic to gain market share via improved customer satisfaction; namely, improve the documentation. Here was a superior customer service need that was going unmet.

In recent years, the machine shop industry in this country has declined, and much of the business has gone overseas. Foreign competition was killing them, and a major supplier of equipment came to us and asked us to conduct some research into the problem.

We began with a series of questions that revealed an interesting statistic: 25% of machine shops in the

United States don't follow recommended oil change guidelines established by the OEM. Clearly, that statistic alone could account for some of the quality problems the industry was experiencing.

By itself, however, that statistic doesn't suggest a route to improve customer satisfaction other than the general imperative of changing oil more frequently.

So we started probing. The first obvious question was: Why don't you change the oil more frequently?

The oft-repeated answer: We think it's just a ploy to sell more oil.

More questions revealed underlying attitudes. First, many machine shops responded that they change the oil when it smells rancid.

"But it doesn't turn rancid all at once," our researcher countered, "it fails over time. And an improperly oiled machine can't hold tolerances and spec required for jobs you're doing."

A number of machine shop foremen said, "If it falls out of spec, we stop the run, tighten it up and run it until it falls out of spec again."

The researcher queried: "But if it only fell out of spec once a week instead of three times a shift, wouldn't that improve productivity?"

"Hey," one machine shop foreman answered, "I got five guys in my maintenance crew. If you take it down to once a week, then I only need one guy."

That was the critical piece of information that we needed. To many machine shop foremen, the failures caused by not changing the oil allowed them to keep people employed. To meet the superior need of this particular internal customer, therefore, the key was separating the employment issue from the productivity one. Any other tactic would be doomed.

DOING THINGS BACKWARDS

More often than not, companies conduct research to learn what went wrong. After-the-fact research is the most common type of research in this country. Typically, a product or service is introduced and falls short of objectives; or there's a significant drop in performance. Management responds by conducting research into the problem, trying to correct the flaw. Of course, the horse has already left the barn.

It is far better if research is conducted proactively,

Figure 1.4   Alternative Research Approaches Exist

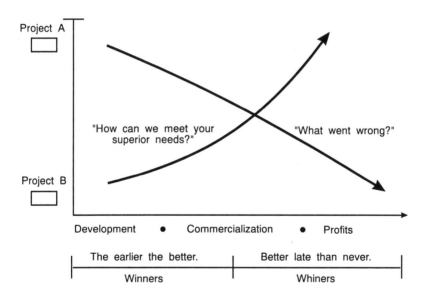

not reactively. But proactive studies are rare—at least the types of studies that set parameters (see Figure 1.4).

Before introducing a product, a company might consider asking the following questions:

- ♦ Would you be willing to pay $___ for this type of product?

- ♦ If we added feature x, would you be willing to pay 15% more?

- ♦ If we doubled the original price, what features would provide you with the payback necessary to buy the product.

Answers to these open-ended questions set parameters. You'll gather information that defines in detail the customer satisfaction requirements of your market. A superior need may emerge.

Does such an approach strike you as too "soft and fuzzy"? I've encountered a prejudice against research that doesn't consist of hard, numerical data gathered from a "statisically significant" audience. The prejudice is a result of tradition. For years, our corporations have depended on direct mail surveys that require yes and no answers. They're easy to interpret and serve as solid justifications for whatever move a company is considering.If the move doesn't pan out, the manager who initiated the move can always point to the hard research and say, "We believed the numbers."

But numbers can lie, and open-ended research can reveal the lie. More importantly, it can also reveal the truth. Nothing is more enlightening than a verbatim from an interviewee. More than once, I've encountered clients skeptical of this type of research. But when I share the verbatims with them, it's like magic. As they pore over the actual words of interview subjects, their eyes light up, and what was formerly just a statistic suddenly becomes flesh and blood.

One of our clients, Kenall Manufacturing, turned a startling piece of information gleaned from open-ended interviews into a highly successful marketing strategy. Since the late 1950s, Kenall has been the leader in the vandal-proof lighting fixture category. But around 1985, sales flattened. Kenall couldn't figure out what was wrong—they were still the market leader, their product quality and service were high, and the demand for vandal-proof lighting was as strong if not stronger than ever.

Then they listened to the voice of the customer. They learned that the market had changed—the traditional customers such as public housing, mental health facilities, and city governments still existed, but new customer segments had emerged. College dormitories, schools, and recreation centers all expressed a superior need for this type of lighting. The problem, they found out, was that architects designing these facilities were reluctant to designate vandal-proof lighting in their plans; they seemed to feel that such a designation might offend their clients.

Armed with this information, Kenall changed the descriptive name of their product to "high-abuse" lighting. With that name change and accompanying marketing efforts, Kenall redefined and reinvigorated their business.

BUT MY COMPANY BELIEVES IN CUSTOMER SATISFACTION

Unfortunately, belief isn't enough. Let's take a typical salesperson for your organization. He's meeting with a customer, and the customer tells him that your company's product would be of greater interest to him if you added feature y. The salesperson immediately thinks: how am I going to overcome that objection and sell what I have to offer today. Your organization is probably like most organizations; it's set up for short-term profit rather than long-term objectives. Your salesperson isn't even concerned with documenting a customer's suggestion; he's concerned with making the sale.

This orientation costs your organization the lead time necessary to comply with a customer's requirements. It also slaps away the customer's implied offer of a "partnership" relationship. Your company may fervently desire this lead time and partnership relationship, but what it wants and what it does are two entirely different matters.

An organization has to back up its belief with action. Recently, our firm undertook an initiative for a Fortune 500 corporation. When we finished the assignment, we had a follow-up meeting with our contact. The contact, a top-level executive, wasn't completely happy; he was concerned about a number of loose ends related to the assignment. The loose ends weren't major; most of them could be traced to a mid-course change in direction issued by the client.

We could have responded by defending our approach; we could have said that most of the issues were relatively minor; we could have pointed to the mid-course change as the root of the problems.

But we did none of those things. Instead, we told our contact—point blank and without qualifications— that we would work on each issue until it was resolved to his total satisfaction and that we would do so without charge.

At first, the executive was dumbfounded. He said, "I have to tell you, I didn't look forward to this meeting; I expected a confrontation. But you're telling me that you're going to resolve all these things?"

We explained that's exactly what we were going to do.

Metra would like to welcome you and your family to our service!

Here are some safety tips for an enjoyable ride. Please:

- Stand well behind the yellow safety line on platforms.

- Keep young children seated with you and instruct them to stay with you at all times, particularly when you are boarding and exiting the train.

- Keep strollers and packages out of the aisle in order to avoid tripping hazards.

- Ask the on-board personnel for assistance if necessary. While they have responsibilities throughout the train, they will make every effort to assist you.

- Be prepared to disembark upon arrival at your destination.

- In order to promote family travel, we have special rates for families and children. We hope you enjoy your ride with us.

If you have any comments or questions, please call **Metra Passenger Services at (312) 322-6777 or RTA Transit Information at 836-7000 (city and suburbs), TTY (312) 836-4949.**

Metra
The way to really fly.

"Well," he said, "I'm speechless. I'm also very pleased."

In a short time, we resolved all the issues that had been troubling our client. Our contact soon became one of our biggest boosters within his organization, telling the story of our meeting to everyone who would listen.

My point is that meeting a superior need is not a static process. You have to change your approach constantly to keep up with evolving customer wants and desires. You can't merely give lip service to customer satisfaction. You have to have a true understanding of your customers and a sufficiently flexible structure to respond to them.

How are you doing so far? To find out, take the following Superior Need Survey.

SUPERIOR NEED SURVEY—WHAT'S YOUR CUSTOMER SATISFACTION SCORE?

As a closed-end survey, the following won't give you a definitive answer. But it will give you a good indication if your approach to customer satisfaction is in line (or out of line) with your customers' superior needs.

When answering the test questions, be aware that there aren't any "wrong" answers—there is simply one answer that is more indicative of a superior need approach than others.

1. Your company has created an image for itself based on:

    A. The historical nature of the company

    B. The superior quality of the company's products and services

C.   The corporate culture

D.   Positive reinforcement of customer images
      related to your product or service

2. If you were asked to define your organization's
    customer, would you define that customer in terms
    of:

    A.   Demographics

    B.   Psychographics

    C.   Needs and expectations

    D.   How your customer compares and
          contrasts to competitors' customers

3. When looking into the future, how far in advance
    do you try to look to determine your customers'
    changing needs?

    A.   One month

    B.   One year

    C.   Three years

    D.   Five years

4. What do you feel is the best way to keep a
    customer satisfied?

    A.   Producing the highest quality products and
          services possible

    B.   Continually questioning and anticipating
          the customer's changing needs, values and
          attitudes

    C.   Constantly improving and upgrading customer service standards

    D.   Providing good products and services at competitive prices

5.   To maintain and improve product quality, you:

    A.   Meet the specs common to your industry

    B.   Meet a series of specs that others often ignore but you feel are important to your particular customer base

    C.   Rely on research and development to improve a product's technology

    D.   Introduce new products in anticipation of new trends

6.   A key factor in meeting customer delivery requirements is:

    A.   Finding and adhering to the time frame that is ideally suited to your customers' needs

    B.   Delivering faster than all competitors

    C.   Creating the perception that your delivery is faster than others

    D.   Avoiding delivery mistakes—wrong product, wrong address, etc.—that cause customers to complain

7.   Your organization responds to emergencies by:

    A.   Doing everything possible to limit the damage caused by the emergency

B.   Implementing a contingency plan designed for all types of emergencies

C.   Finding a way to turn an emergency into an opportunity for better customer relationships

D.   Dealing honestly and quickly with the customer problems caused by the emergency

8.   What factor has the greatest impact on the pricing of your products and services?

A.   Pre-determined profit margin

B.   Competitors' pricing

C.   The perceived (by customers) value of your product or service

D.   The manufacturing and other associated costs to bring your product or service to market

9.   Your research and development group is driven by:

A.   Practical and theoretical suggestions from customers

B.   Hard statistical market data

C.   Other executives, especially those in sales and marketing

D.   Ideas from the R&D department.

10. To assess the level of customer satisfaction among your company's customers, you rely primarily on which of the following for your assessment:

A. Intuition

B. Input from front-line employees (salespeople)

C. Closed-ended research (yes-no formatted questions)

D. Open-ended research (respondents are asked a series of questions with no limitation on their answers)

11. Your customer service department solves problems by:

A. Moving as quickly as possible to identify and correct the source of the problem

B. Making customers part of the solution

C. Creating a constant dialog with customers that creates the perception that the company is concerned with their needs

D. Developing a marketing program that communicates the company's emphasis on a high level of customer service

12. What is the most important information you know about your three top competitors?

A. Their market share

B. Their plans to expand their share and pirate customers away from your company in the coming year

C. How their customer relationships compare and contrast with those of your company

    D.   The new technologies, services, and products that they're developing and plan to introduce soon

13. If you could magically look into your customer's mind and extract any type of information, would it be:

    A.   The thing he or she most likes about your company's products and services

    B.   What would cause the customer to stop buying from your company and buy from a competitor

    C.   What that customer values about your products and services now, and what he or she would value in the future

    D.   The perception he or she has about your company

14. How do you go about converting noncustomers to customers?

    A.   Primarily through comparative advertising, hard-hitting direct mail, and price promotions

    B.   By researching the underlying reasons why non-customers prefer your competitors and what it would take to make them change their minds

    C.   Through target marketing that is tailored to what you believe a given market segment will respond to

    D.   Through new product or service introductions or improvements that will open up new markets

ANSWERS

1. D 2. C 3. D 4. B 5. B 6. A 7. C 8. C 9. A
10. D 11. B 12. C 13. C 14. B

SCORING

12 or more correct answers: **SATISFACTION GUARANTEED**

7-11 correct answers: **ON RIGHT TRACK, BUT ROOM FOR IMPROVEMENT**

4-6 correct answers: **MEDIOCRE**

3 or fewer correct answers: **POOR**

Chapter 2

Satisfied Today, Dissatisfied Tomorrow

W hat have you done for me lately?" has been the rallying cry of customers since the street peddler started selling his wares. No matter how loyal a company's customers were, all it took was for a problem to evolve in product quality or for a competitor to sell something at a lower price, and that customer asked his question.

Today, however, the stakes are higher. In the past, customers were more forgiving. They had fewer options. Your organization had fewer competitors. You could fail to satisfy the customer and the mistake wasn't fatal. You'd get another chance to win back a customer.

Now, there are no second chances. Global competition has raised the stakes. You lose a customer once, you lose him for a long time. No one knows this lesson better than U.S. automobile manufacturers.

Satisfying the superior need is the answer to "what have you done for me lately?" But most organizations find it difficult to provide that answer. To begin with, they're not structured to do so.

THE ARCHAIC PYRAMID

Companies still labor under a pyramid structure. It's a time-tested, familiar structure. For years, it worked well, providing a logic to corporate organizations. Like its military counterpart, it allowed messages to be passed down from the top and carried out by ever-widening layers of subordinates. It ensured that orders were obeyed.

But it took a long time to work. A bank finds that customers are complaining about a new checking account; it seems that the minimum balance is too high, and customers are also angry about the $25 service charge if the account dips below the minimum. The complaints crawl up the pyramid structure of the bank like a worm up a mountain. When the president is finally informed of the problem, he says, "Let's have a meeting about this." Seven key executives are asked to come to the meeting, and it takes weeks before everyone can clear a time to meet—there are far more immediate concerns, like launching a new advertising campaign and restructuring the operations department. At the meeting, the problem is discussed. It's decided that a committee should be appointed to formulate a course of action. More weeks pass as the committee is assembled and as they map out a solution.

The committee makes a presentation to the president, who likes the solution: setting up an alternative checking account with a lower minimum balance and service charge for customers and phasing out the one that customers dislike.

A plan is created to introduce the alternative account to customers. Every division is informed of the plan and how to implement it. Instructions are given to operations, public relations, advertising, and customer service managers. They, in turn, tell their assistants who, in turn, communicate instructions to their subordinates. By the time the plan is implemented, the bank has lost a significant number of accounts.

Now, imagine if the bank has a cluster structure; namely, small, tight-knit groups of people with decision-making ability as well as with a direct line to customers. Within a matter of days, they'd be able to respond to customer complaints with a new and improved checking account system.

Clusters are the wave of the future. When they'll break on the shore of traditional American corporations is another matter. Not only do you have all managers with vested interest in the pyramid, but you also have the enormous financial and reorganizational issues to confront. As the Egyptians understand, pyramids take a long time to build and they don't come down easily (see Figure 2.1).

MOVING UP THE PYRAMID

As difficult as it is to get a message to flow down the pyramid, it's even more difficult to get a customer's message to flow up—especially one that relates to the superior need, which isn't as obvious as lesser or more established needs. It's a steep ascent over smooth, sloping walls, and there's nothing for that voice to hang on to. While the CEO's directives are pushed down through the sheer power of the CEO's voice, the customer's voice is small and weak. It's easy for that voice to stop at the customer service department and never go any higher. There's the presumption that a

Figure 2.1   Organizational Structure Affects Responsiveness

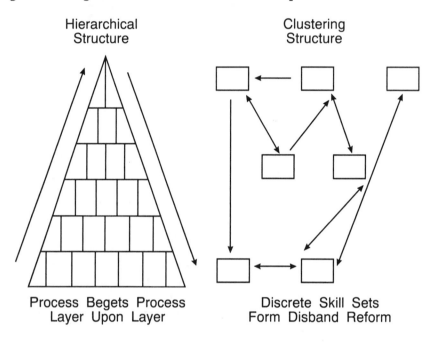

"higher-up" need not be bothered with such trivial matters. Or the complaint the voice makes is shuttled to a committee or task force for study, remaining in that middle-level limbo. It's not that organizations intentionally want to be unresponsive to customers; it's simply that they don't have the structure to be responsive.

At some point, there's an intersection between the voice of the customer moving up and orders from top management moving down. When the two voices meet, the place that they meet is often "middle management." It's at this point that customer satisfaction hangs in the balance. An opportunity exists here for recognizing and acting upon a compelling customer need. If someone doesn't step forward and propose and implement an action in response to the customer's need, dissatisfaction is likely.

No question, it's difficult for middle management to assume this risk. If you're in a pyramid organization, you could well be risking your job if you decide to go forward and circumvent the layers above you to meet customer needs. But if your program works—if you satisfy the customer and your efforts impact on the bottom line—good things will follow (see Figure 2.2).

More than ever before, our organizations require people to step forward and take customer satisfaction risks. If we simply maintain the status quo, customer dissatisfaction will continue to rise at an alarming rate.

Figure 2.2   **Where Process Meets Potential and Compelling Customer Need is Intercepted and Acted Upon**

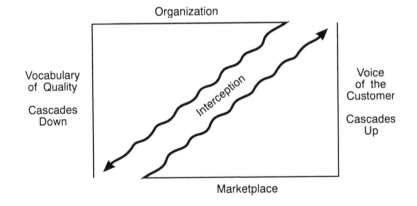

You can bet that the companies introducing new high-speed railroads in this country won't maintain the status quo. The intersection between the voice of the customer moving up and orders from top management moving down is evident in the bold plans of these companies. Just as airlines took passenger business away from railroads years ago, the train companies are about to return the favor. They listened to the customer and heard complaints about airline arrogance, about lack of comfort, about flight delays and safety problems. They heard about baggage that wasn't delivered to the right place and horrible traffic tie-ups going to and from airports. Top management of high-speed railroads were undeterred by the old argument that the transportation race goes to the swiftest; they're willing to gamble on the emerging superior need of increased comfort, reliability and safety; that consumers will sacrifice a little speed for those benefits.

RISING EXPECTATIONS

Computerization and other technological breakthroughs have raised customer expectations sky-high. Combined with sophisticated marketing and extensive media coverage of new developments, the average customer expects a level of speed, quality, and reliability that is beyond the means of most organizations.

In addition, the world is changing. New cultural and social trends and a volatile economy impact customer attitudes and norms. The pace of change is fast, and it's difficult for companies to keep up with the ways those changes affect their customers.

When videocassette recorders were first introduced to the consumer market, they were bulky, expensive products that were difficult to use and limited in their features. People who bought them were the affluent few, and they expected only to have a machine with which they could play rented movies. A few years later, everything changed. Now, the bulk of the population expects to pay around $200 for a good unit; they expect remote control and recording features; they expect high-quality reproduction; they expect to have the choice of numerous premium features such as multiple-event programming and stereo sound.

The same rising expectations have occurred in the automobile market. Until recently, a given model changed very little from year to year; it usually took ten years for significant changes to become standard. Now, the rate of change—and corresponding customer expectations—have accelerated at a frightening pace. People expect each new model to offer more and better features. Everyone assumes that automatic transmission, air-conditioning, stereo-radio and many other features will be standard. They demand options such as CD players, anti-lock brakes, and airbags.

What can a company do to meet these rising expectations? Given limited resources, how can an organization satisfy customer demands without going broke?

The first step is to pinpoint the right customer.

LOOKING FOR MR. AND MRS. RIGHT

If your organization is typical, it has numerous customer segments. Using computer technology, you've defined those segments via a sophisticated database that incorporates demographics and psychographics.

In the past, you probably could serve these multiple segments. Today, with customer expectations soaring and competition intensifying, it's become much more difficult. The odds are that your company is much better able to serve some segments than others. If you were to conduct a survey, you'd probably find that your scores were very high among certain segments and very low among others.

You have two choices. You can try and improve your scores where you've done poorly. Or you can focus on the segments where you're strong and likely to remain so.

I realize this second option is a difficult one to swallow. For years, American corporations have emphasized diversity, expanding markets, and targeting emerging segments. To narrow one's focus is a bitter pill.

But, hold your nose and take it. Customer satisfaction will come to those companies that narrow their strategies and meet the superior need of a specialized audience rather than meeting secondary needs of a broader market.

The best analogy to illustrate this philosophy is cable's remarkable success. Broadcast networks— ABC, CBS and NBC—send their signals out to everyone, fulfilling their role as a mass medium. For a long time, they were able to satisfy their customers. But technology created new possibilities and eventually, rising expectations. Television viewers became aware that they didn't have to wait until the evening news to find out what was happening in the world; they could find a recent movie without waiting for prime time to roll around; and that they could watch a great college basketball game on days other than Saturday.

Cable's narrowcasting formula was an idea whose time had come. Each station had a much smaller audience than one of the big-three networks. But they were able to satisfy that audience far better than a broadcast network. Cable meets its customers' superior need for specialized programming far better than any broadcast station.

Catalog houses like Lands End and Spiegel, retailers like The Gap and The Limited, and food companies like Celestial Seasonings and Ben and Jerry's have all become companies that have satisfied their customer segments with their "narrowcast" strategies.

Big, "broadcast" corporations can follow this example. American Express, for instance, has taken a step in this direction by sending mailings to credit card customers offering them a selection of 50 products that they can purchase at favorable prices. By itself, there's nothing special about this tactic. What makes it special is how American Express chooses the items; they conduct a computer analysis of purchases made by customers using their credit cards and determine the key items they're buying. It's a terrific way to target their customers' needs and build a secondary profit center.

In the future, it wouldn't surprise me if American Express limits use of their credit cards to a select group of customers. There will be only platinum cards, and to qualify for one you have to have a certain income level. Perhaps that seems a fanciful notion now. But in the near future, it may be the only way that American Express can keep its customers satisfied, especially if competitors offer dramatically lower credit card interest rates.

THE INTERNAL CUSTOMER

Simply narrowing your market focus isn't enough to ensure superior need satisfaction. It certainly won't be enough if you neglect the "internal customer."

Most organizations claim to train their people in meeting customer needs in the following ways:

   ◆ They establish customer service departments;

♦ Institute programs designed to find new
  ways to handle customer complaints;

♦ Conduct research to determine where they're
  falling short; and

♦ Create slogans revolving around "The customer is always right" to keep "top-of-mind"
  awareness of this priority.

Yet, they fall short of the goal. The problem is
what I call the Perception Gap: the gulf between the
employees' understanding of what an organization
preaches and what it practices. Too often, companies
underestimate what it will take to make their people
proficient at understanding and responding to the
needs of customers. Sometimes, they provide their
people with customer satisfaction programs but not
the tools to provide it. Sometimes, they inadvertently
force employees to work with contradictory policies.
Do everything possible to please an unhappy customer, but never give a refund without clearing it with
two superiors and receiving permission in writing.

Most importantly, organizations fail to give employees the flexibility and freedom to use their common sense in situations where time and creativity are
required to satisfy customers. Management doesn't
recognize that each customer is different, and that
each has his or her own set of priorities, problems, and
needs. A uniform policy will not satisfy each and every
customer.

When the internal customer isn't satisfied, relationships with the external customer suffer. Nothing
illustrates this point better than an experience I recently had searching for a camera for my wife's birthday.

I decided to try shopping for the camera at the
new WalMart that had just opened near my home. I'd
read all the great publicity the company had received;
my expectations had been raised by their spectacular

growth, by their low prices, and by Sam Walton's commitment to his customers.

As I walked to the store, I was impressed by the beautiful building and the abundant, convenient parking. The store's inside was equally impressive. It was well-organized, bright and attractively designed. A salesperson helpfully told me that I could purchase a camera at two locations in the store: the photo section or the electronics section. I went to the photo section first. The salesman directed me to a display case with a variety of cameras, priced from $50 to $500.

"What's the difference between the high-priced and low-priced cameras?" I asked him.

The salesman removed the two cameras, examined them quizzically, shook his head and tried, "Features?"

I decided to try electronics.

There, the display was much more extensive and attractive. I told this salesperson that I was looking for a $200 camera. He pointed me toward a guide the size of a telephone book bolted to a counter five yards away from the camera display. After 45 minutes of reading and moving back and forth between the display and the guide, I found a camera that seemed appropriate. I asked the salesman if I could examine it.

After a few minutes of searching, he told me that he didn't have it. In fact, he didn't have a single camera listed in the guide.

I walked over to the service desk and asked to see the manager.

"Can I tell him what this is about?" the woman at the service desk asked me.

At this point, I was more than a little peeved and said, "No, you can't."

Before the manager appeared, two store security personnel walked by, inspecting me at the request of the service desk woman, I assumed. This also did not sit well with me. Did every request to see the store manager require such an inspection?

When the manager came out, I explained what had happened. After some hemming and hawing, he said, "You know, this isn't a great time to buy a camera. The inventory is being worked down, and they haven't loaded the inventory for next season. That's why we have some of the cameras but none of the literature about them, and why the literature we have is for cameras we don't carry anymore."

"How long does this go on?"

"Another few months," he replied.

"What if I wanted to buy a video camera or a CD player?"

"It would probably be the same situation," he admitted.

I left without a camera and no intention of ever returning.

In this store, at least, WalMart failed to meet the needs of its internal customer. The first salesman lacked the training to help me differentiate a low-priced camera from a high-priced one. The second salesman had not been informed that inventory for cameras listed in the guide didn't exist, and he had a display area where the guide was located too far away from the merchandise.

The manager was playing his role by the book. He was adhering to the "honesty is the best policy" of the company; he was courteous and responsive to my questions. But he lacked the training and the authority to show any initiative to solve a customer problem.

He should have asked my name and for whom I was buying the camera; he should have invited me to his office for a cup of coffee so we could discuss the situation and find a solution.

He should have said, "Mr. Lytle, I'm troubled by what you've told me. Why don't we go to the camera department, where you can show me the one camera in which you're interested. I'll make it my business to get that camera, with flash and film. I'll have it couriered from another store and have it at your house by tomorrow morning."

That would have satisfied me. My superior need was relatively simple: I wanted a little bit of comparative information, a camera with certain features in a certain price range, and fast delivery. Though that need could not be met when I walked into the store, there was an opportunity to meet it later. The manager should have listened to his "research"—the need that I was communicating—and responded creatively to it. It is what I—and what most other customers—expect.

Is this realistic? Do we expect too much? Not at all. Think about all the money WalMart has spent on building the store, advertising it, training its people and so forth. A customer comes into the store and wants to give them his money, and all that is required to conclude that transaction is a minute or two of personal attention to a very specific customer need. We should expect nothing less, and any company that doesn't think such a response is realistic had better educate itself about the new reality.

Maybe in the past, I would have made allowances. I would have assumed that I'd be giving up a certain amount of service by shopping at a discounter. Not today. Today, there are too many other shopping options available. I, like many other customers, will choose them without a second thought.

THE NECESSARY COMMITMENT

If you don't want the result to be customers like me who vow never to buy from a particular company again, you need to raise your customer service policies and practices to a higher level; namely, a superior need level. To do this takes the nerve of a riverboat gambler.

You're going to have to do things your company has never done before, and that's scary. Invariably, it's going to be a rocky road.

Morton International has a polysulfide-based raw material with a number of valuable properties as a sealant. For many years, Morton did extremely well in the sealant market, establishing a leadership position. Then, the market peaked and began a decline. Through no fault of their own, Morton found itself with a material that was no longer as profitable as it once had been.

Typically, a company will accept this situation as inevitable and simply manage the downward spiral as best it can. But Morton was sufficiently courageous that they wanted to hear the bad news from the customer himself, not just from numbers contained in financial reports. They took a chance and invested in a search for the superior customer need relative to their material. Was there a market out there that they hadn't explored and for whom their material solved a critical problem? Was there a way of reinvigorating their traditional markets, perhaps by reformulating the material? There were many questions asked, and the answers were valuable. Morton found not one but many opportunities for their raw material, unearthing superior needs in different market segments. For instance, they found that polysulfide met an emerging need for protecting the environment from chemical and petroleum spills. Acting quickly and decisively to meet that need, Morton has established a ground floor position in a socially desirable growth market.

Hewlett Packard is another company that's trying to move to a superior customer need level. They've made a commitment to have the highest "freshness" of product in every market. To live up to that commitment, they're rolling out any product that passes the following test. It must have two definable feature differences (and accompanying customer benefits) from other competitive products. To make such a strategy financially feasible, they produce only enough product to cover demand so they're not left with huge inventories if the product fails. If it does fail, they take it off the market. It it succeeds, they rev up production.

The jury's still out on HP. But no one can question their level of commitment. If it pays off, they'll achieve unprecedented customer satisfaction scores. Certainly, they're taking a risk, but it's a risk that's accompanied by the possibility of tremendous rewards.

CAN YOU ANSWER THESE QUESTIONS TO YOUR SATISFACTION?

Do your customers fall into the satisfied today, dissatisfied tomorrow category? To get a sense if that's the case, consider the following checklist in light of your organization:

___1. Has there been a major external change—cultural, technological, social, economic—that has decreased your customers' satisfaction with your company's products or services?

___2. Does your company operate with a traditional pyramid structure; and if so, do you find that it's unable to respond promptly to customer concerns?

___3. Have specific events—a competitor's new product introduction, news of a breakthrough in your industry—created rising expectations among your customers that are beyond your organization's capacity to meet?

___4. Looking at your customer base, are there segments that your company is significantly less adept at serving than others?

__5. Do you feel that your internal customer—the entire employee population—has all the tools, the knowledge, and the motivation necessary to fulfill your company's mission of customer satisfaction?

__6. Has your company made a total commitment to revamp its approach to customer satisfaction in the 1990s, to pull out all the stops to meet the superior customer need?

The answers to the checklist don't have to be definitive; they're simply designed to give you a reading of how your company is responding to the radical changes and growing customer expectations of this decade. If your company is like most organizations, you'll find that you come up short—that your organization is still laboring under a 1980s mindset, aspiring to quality status yet unable to take the leap of faith required.

If so, there's a solution. It begins with knowing the customer by more than his or her demographic statistics.

DEVELOPING MUTUALLY BENEFICIAL RELATIONSHIPS

Does your organization have a relationship with its customers that goes beyond buy and sell?

By definition, a "relationship" is personal. It assumes not only familiarity, but also an intimate sense of the other person, and a recognition of and response to that person's likes and dislikes, dreams, and desires.

Creating such a relationship is impossible if you don't know your customer—or if you know him or her only through the surface data that most closed-ended market research produces.

The EMS/PerformancePlus method is designed to lay the groundwork for such a relationship. It is an interactive, strategic approach to market research that yields superior need information (and will be explained in more detail in the next chapter). No matter how sophisticated your marketing tools or how state-of-the-art your information-gathering technology, this open-ended research method yields far more information than you presently possess. In short, it probes below the surface of your customers' vital statistics.

I had one client that was shocked to learn that a market segment believed that their new and improved two-day delivery service wasn't fast enough; that customers expected overnight service for one particular product category. I had another client that was surprised to learn that their definition of quality and their customers' definition of quality were far apart. Customers measured quality based on five factors, while the client had only considered one of the factors. Yet another client discovered that a significant percentage of customers considered them an unreliable supplier, despite the fact that a recent industry survey had ranked them number one in terms of reliability. (EMS/PerformancePlus revealed that customers found them reliable during slow business periods and unreliable during hectic times when customers considered reliability most important.)

This type of information lets organizations understand what customers really care about. In many instances, customers may have never articulated these concerns or communicated them properly. How does this knowledge translate into avoiding the satisfied today, dissatisfied tomorrow syndrome?

By giving you "inside" information. It's similar to an investor who learns that a company is going to be acquired and immediately buys shares in that company. In other words, you're able to anticipate where the customer is heading before he gets there.

What if McDonald's learned that—contrary to their assumptions—their customers liked the taste of high-fat burgers? Although they may have responded to a survey by indicating their desire for a low-fat alternative, they actually would never purchase a less-tasty low-fat one.

What if Apple Computer discovered that price wasn't a factor in their target market's decision to buy Apple versus IBM; that the real problem was that the company's computer guru actually preferred the higher-priced Macintosh, but he wouldn't switch from IBM because he wasn't convinced Apple was in the business market to stay.

If you aren't aware of these customer "secrets," you're going to be playing catch-up when they're finally revealed.

On the other hand, you don't want to get too far out in front of the customer. If you're way out ahead, you probably won't last until he catches up with you. But once you understand your customers' deepest secrets, you can get a bit ahead, shine a flashlight on the path, and be sure that you're there waiting (with the right products and services) when they get there.

EMS/PerformancePlus enables you to move ahead and helps you to shine the light on the right path. The next chapter details the customer satisfaction methodology available to you. For now, two points are important:

- ♦ Customer satisfaction is a fragile thing, so handle it with care.

- ♦ Customer relationships are built through insight and foresight, not through standard marketing tools.

I'll leave you with one last story. Think about going into a car dealership and looking for a car. Typically, the salesperson questions you about the type of car that you're looking for and what you're willing to spend. Perhaps you test drive a vehicle. You tell him that you like it, and then you engage in a price debate. Typically, you reach a stalemate. He pulls the ploy of having to talk to his boss about lowering the price any further; he leaves and comes back, saying that he can only go down another $100. He says, "Look, we're only a few hundred dollars apart. You don't want to have to go through all this again at another dealership. What do you say?"

In this case, the salesperson hasn't established a relationship with you—at least a relationship in which he demonstrates any real concern for who you are, what you need, how his product will provide you with benefits that are particularly suited to your situation. Even if you decide to buy the car there, you won't feel any particular loyalty to the dealer because the experience was distasteful, and you leave feeling like you've just come off the battlefield.

Now consider what it might have been like if you'd gone to a car dealership with a superior need mindset. The salesperson greeted you when you came in and asked you to sit down with him to discuss your transportation needs. He said, "Before showing you any of our cars, let's talk about the type of purchase that's going to make sense for you. I'd like to ask you a few questions that will help you make that determination:

- ◆ Can you tell me if this is going to be your only car?

- ◆ Who in your family is going to drive it? Are you going to use it for business?

- ◆ Have you thought about leasing instead of buying?

- ◆ Do you want a used car instead of a new one? If you want to wait two months, we're going to be getting our new models in, and they all

have airbags as standard equipment, so if
that's a concern . . ."

For a large organization, forming solid customer
relationships is a bit more difficult than it is for a
salesperson at a car dealership. But the philosophy
behind the approach to the customer remains the
same. If you can learn the customers' needs and tailor
every facet of your business to those needs, then your
market will be satisfied today and satisfied tomorrow.

Chapter 3

The Voice of the Customer

J ust about every organization puts its ear to the marketplace and tries to hear their customers' voices. They hope for a clear, happy, and singular response. However, what they get is a tower of babble.

That's to be expected. Every organization will have customers with myriad attitudes about the organization, its products, and its services. Even companies with relatively homogeneous markets will find wildly different customer perspectives, needs, and demands.

There's an almost desperate quality to an organization's attempts to make sense of customers' voices. The desperation is justified. After all, with millions of present and prospective customers spread over a huge geographic area, listening for something intelligible and useful can be difficult.

Yet, it's necessary. Few companies today are so arrogant that they believe that they can create demand for their products and services and that they, not the customer, know best. If they can get a reading of their customers' likes and dislikes, needs and expectations, then they can compete. If they can identify that one need that rises above the others, then they can win.

In their desperate quest for the voice, companies rush into their markets with the tool they understand best: traditional market research. Subsequently, they hire a market research firm to do closed-end direct mail surveys that ask people to check boxes. The results are then tabulated, analyzed, and translated into marketing.

Most companies realize that it is not the greatest way to reveal the customer voice. However, they rationalize that it's better than nothing and indicates something.

Not necessarily. More often than not, such research paints a false picture. It's just one of the mistakes organizations make in their fevered attempts to hear their customers' voices. Before examining the correct techiques to capture those voices, let's look at some common mistakes.

MISTAKE #1: Trusting Closed-Ended Research to Provide Anything More Than a Numerical Glimpse of the Voice

Many organizations make crucial marketing decisions based on pure statistics. For example, 40% of customers would buy product A if it contained feature 3; 75% of customers are dissatisfied with our service speed.

In response, companies add feature 3 and increase their service speed.

I'm oversimplifying, but you get the point. Closed-ended research is inaccurate for a number of the following reasons.

The answers are black and white. There's no room to get a reading of the grey areas, the subtleties, and the nuances that really define "customer voice." When you're limited to "yes" and "no," to multiple choice, and to assigning a numerical value between one and five, you miss the *how, what, why, where and when.*

The surveys are answered by the wrong people. The CEO passes his survey on to an administrative assistant to fill out; the housewife gives it to her husband; and the doctor gives it to his nurse. There's no guarantee that a mailed survey is going to be filled out by the appropriate respondent.

Many surveys are filled out by people who are in the wrong frame of mind. Contrary to what some market researchers would have you believe, respondents don't set aside a block of time and carefully peruse the questions before answering. Typically, they reluctantly steal a minute or two from a busy day and rush through the answers like it was some sort of meaningless test. An impersonal piece of mail doesn't give many people a vested interest in providing thoughtful responses.

MISTAKE #2: **Misinterpreting What You Think the Voice Is Saying**

If only the voice spoke in simple English. Unfortunately, the voice can say one thing, but it can mean something else entirely. If you interpret it solely on instinct—even if it's a CEO's instinct—miscommunication will likely result.

I was recently aboard American Airlines when I picked up their in-flight magazine. An editorial by CEO Robert Crandall responded to customer complaints about limited legroom. In his well-written editorial, Mr. Crandall explained why it was impossible for American to provide more legroom. He cited statistics that showed increased legroom would result in decreased seating per plane which was an economic handicap. He also referred to a study that showed additional legroom would not enhance customer loyalty. Therefore, eliminating a given number of seats in favor of more space for passengers' legs would put American at a competitive disadvantage.

I applaud Mr. Crandall for addressing this delicate issue. He correctly assumed that it was an issue that concerned his customers. He incorrectly assumed that economic hardship was an excuse that would satisfy his customers.

As I read Mr. Crandall's editorial, my 6'2" frame was scrunched into a very small space. I was not satisfed with what he had to say. He was assuming that I only wanted an explanation for the problem, and that an explanation would be sufficient. It wasn't. I wanted to know if they were exploring ways to solve the problem. I would have been satisfied by some indication that an effort was being made to solve the problem.

Is my view shared by the majority of Mr. Crandall's other passengers? It might be wise to find out, rather than making assumptions about the customer voice.

MISTAKE #3: **Listening to the Voice Only Through Qualitative, In-Person Research**

Focus groups and one-on-one interviews are two common examples of qualitative research. (I have and will use the terms "open-ended" and "interactive" as synonyms for qualitative.) Unlike closed ended mail surveys, they offer the advantages of open-ended questions and answers and in-depth probing.

But they're limited in providing useful information about the customer voice. The following problems exist:

Much of the information gained is of the "soft and fuzzy" variety. You receive a report from your qualitative research firm that contains scores of verbatims—transcripts of their responses. You are also given the benefit of the research firm's conclusions. For instance, "Respondents overwhelmingly found Company X's products to be durable and of high quality." More than one corporate executive has looked at these results and asked, "What does all this mean?" It's very difficult to translate the information gained from one-on-ones into effective strategies and tactics. It tends to lack focus, because the responses and the questions that evoked the responses aren't framed by a scientific structure. Respondent answers are so subjective that it's difficult to draw any conclusions.

The sample size is small. Unless you have a huge budget and a great deal of time, it's difficult to conduct the number of one-on-ones required to obtain sufficient data. This is especially true when the targeted customer base is large and heterogeneous.

The respondents' answers are coded in a simple, undifferentiated way. Many qualitative research firms lump responses into broad categories; they fail to break out sub-segments of a category. For instance, 34% of one-on-ones say that quality is the primary factor in their most recent purchasing decisions. But their coding doesn't reveal that 12% believe quality means durability; 20% believe it means serviceability; and 2% believe it means reliability.

A DIRECT CONNECTION TO THE CUSTOMER VOICE

The telephone is an instrument designed to hear a voice. It has the advantage of speed over paper research and one-on-ones. More importantly, it has the capability to create a meaningful dialog between interviewer and interviewee. In many ways, it's better suited to this goal than one-on-ones. In personal interviews, the interview subject is easily distracted. (Ironically, the distraction is often a phone call). The actual presence of an interviewer can be a negative factor. The subject doesn't have the necessary distance from the interviewer to reflect and contemplate.

Still, the telephone will only lead to the voice if it's used properly. Many telemarketers use it improperly. In the wrong hands, it becomes an intrusive, irritating communication vehicle. Rude, robotic, and rambling interviewers—combined with a poorly designed research/evaluation system—will yield nothing of value.

Through our extensive use of the Performance-Plus system over many years, we've found that certain techniques are critical for capturing the customer voice. Let's examine those techniques and how you can use them.

UNDERSTANDING THE ENVIRONMENT

When you call a customer and request information, you're going to be met by a defense system. If you can't penetrate it, you'll either fail to elicit any information, or the response you get will be incomplete or just plain wrong. Finding the superior need can't be accomplished without the cooperation and enthusiasm of your customer-interviewee. That's why you need to be aware of the defense system that discourages cooperation and enthusiasm.

The defense system consists of equal parts

♦ Anxiety

♦ Irritation

♦ Reluctance

The "anxiety" stems from fear of the unknown. What does the caller want? Who does he represent? What information will you be asked to provide?

The "irritation" is a product of past experiences. It represents all those obnoxious, unprofessional telemarketing calls and the suspicion that the caller is trying to sell something.

The "reluctance" is a result of not knowing how the information provided will be used. Will it come back to haunt the respondent?

Breaking through this defense system begins with the interviewer's introduction. Here are the checklist elements that should be in every introduction:

CHECKLIST

Introduction

Identify yourself—clearly state who you are, and the company for which you're working. This is common courtesy and something every person you call will expect and appreciate.

Explain the purpose of the call. Don't beat around the bush. Immediately clarify what information you're seeking.

State why you're calling this person specifically.
This is absolutely critical, and it's often overlooked.
People need to understand why they were picked for
the call. If they view your choice as logical and appropriate—if they can nod their head and feel good that
they were chosen—then you'll receive their enthusiastic participation in the process.

The First Question

Many respondents will grudgingly agree to respond.
If you sense some reluctance on the interviewee's part,
never begin with a high-anxiety question. Examples of
this type of question include:

> ◆ How much do you make a year?
>
> ◆ What percentage of your personal income is
>   spent on . . . ?
>
> ◆ Can you afford to spend x dollars on . . . ?
>
> ◆ Does your spouse work?
>
> ◆ Are you satisified with your company's com-
>   puter programs?

Any question that touches a potential contro-
versy should be avoided at first. You'll raise the subject's anxiety level to a point that nothing you do
afterwards will bring it back down.

Therefore, start with a nonthreatening query.
Ask something that is more general than specific and
that leads the person toward where you want to go.
Let's say you own a furniture company and you are
trying to gauge customer perceptions of a particular
line. You might start with: "Can you give me your
definition of quality as it relates to furniture?"

FOLLOW UP WITH A PROBE

No matter how detailed the response, always follow
the first question with a "probe"; that is, a query
designed to elicit a more in-depth explanation of the
initial response. It can be as simple as: "Can you clarify
that list you gave me?" Or: "Are there other points
besides those you've mentioned?"

Such probes serve two purposes. First, they're
part of the conversation dynamic. Reading a scripted
list of questions is an interrogation, not a meaningful
interview. Second, we've found that some of best nuggets of information are buried beneath that first answer. Perhaps the respondent hasn't thought enough
about his answer; perhaps he simply forgot something. Probes dig up those nuggets, and they can be
central to customer concerns.

BUILDING BRIDGES

Many telephone interviewers ask questions in a ran-
dom pattern. They aren't cognizant of the pattern's
effect on the interview subject. Too often, the interview
is stilted and uncomfortable; there's no attempt to
establish a dialog.

One way a dialog can be established is by using
"bridge" questions; namely, questions that are not
designed to elicit specific information as much as to
reduce anxiety and to involve the interview subject.

For example, we often incorporate what we like
to call "visionary" questions—ones that invite the interview subject to speculate on future trends. Typically, these questions raise the subject's level of
interest in the conversation, making it easier to follow
up with a more pertinent, high-anxiety query.

An example of a visionary question is: "What's the most unlikely but probable event to occur in your industry?" This question is inherently paradoxical, but that paradox forces people to probe their own thoughts. If you asked this question of an automobile executive, he might respond, "Well, eventually we'll move to hovercraft, which will allow us to replace cement with grass, creating necessary green space and satisfying a host of environmental concerns." That provocative answer might lead you to information about environmental issues that you would otherwise miss. If you require further proof that this type of question is useful, consider what would have happened if you had asked it of a sales manager ten years ago. He might have responded: "This might sound goofy, but with the rapidly rising cost of sales calls, I can see a time when every salesperson has a phone in his or her car." It's quite possible that a cellular phone company heard exactly this response from people they interviewed and captured one of the most significant superior needs to emerge in the last decade.

CONVERSATION STIMULATORS

During the course of asking questions, the interviewer can use a number of devices to keep the dialog going. They include:

Repeating part or all of the subject's response and asking, "Did I get that right, or is there something you want to add?"

Acting the part of a learner, not an expert. Nothing turns an interviewee off faster than "Mr. Know-it-all." When it seems as if the interviewer knows everything, the result is off-putting. The respondent says to himself, "The guy's a jerk" or "He already knows the answers, so why even bother asking me." Therefore, try to convey that you need the respondent's help in educating you. Treat him as the expert. Say, "I'm not clear on this point, can you explain it for me," or "Help me understand this issue."

Responding to the interviewee as a person, not as a question-asking robot. It's okay to respond naturally, to express surprise at an answer, to say you're impressed with an idea, and to laugh at something that's funny. Contrary to popular opinion, you don't taint the "science" of the interview by reacting naturally. More often than not, your genuine responses will increase the likelihood that the respondent will answer more honestly and completely.

THE INTERVIEWER

Never forget this rule: The quality of the responses received is directly proportional to the quality of the person eliciting the responses. Telephone research's weak link is the interviewer. If the person making the call lacks the knowledge, training, talent, and commitment to do a good job, the value of the interview will be lessened. Hiring novices might be cost-effective for a boiler room telemarketing operation, but it's ill-advised if your goal is to conduct a sophisticated marketing interview.

Whoever you choose to conduct phone interviews, they should be professionals—people who are skilled at research, who are adept at talking on the phone, who have a passion to learn, and who have an ability to think on their feet. They should understand and be involved in the process—they should not be "hired hands" whose only skills are asking questions and making "x's" in appropriate boxes.

Test candidates. Observe them during a few practice runs on the telephone. Identify those people who sparkle, who light up like an actor on the stage when they begin talking. It won't be hard to separate the wheat from the chaff. You'll quickly note the individuals who communicate their sense of excitement to the person on the other end of the phone. Eliminate the callers who speak in a monotone and who are at a loss for words when they receive unexpected responses.

Sometimes, the right person for the job is a senior executive, a marketing director, or a high-level manager. Does that strike you as odd? Do you think it's inappropriate for anyone but a functionary to be making these calls?

Then consider how important the information gleaned from these interviews can be to your organization. What you learn can make or break your company in the coming years. Beneath the placid surface of the customer voice are potential resources of great value. Do you want to dig below the surface with a blunt instrument? Or would you rather go at it with a sharp, effective tool? It's a critical job, and no one should feel the task is "beneath" him.

EVALUATING THE RESPONSES

Evaluating the responses is a four-step process. The mountains of information you receive must be broken down and analyzed in a systematic, logical way. If it isn't, you may become the victim of misinterpretation which is the researcher's worst nightmare. Therefore, begin with the following steps:

STEP #1:   INTERVIEWER INPUT. Typically, the person who conducts the interview is cut off from the process as soon as the calls are completed. The idea behind closed cell check boxes is that the interviewer can't shape the answers with his biases.

That's a terrible fallacy. Who is in a better position to interpret someone's responses than the person who asked the questions? During our PerformancePlus process, we always ask our interviewers to spend some time after they're done to go over what they've recorded. We request that they find a quiet place to contemplate the answers. Then, in a "comments" section, they provide their subjective opinions. For instance, "This interviewee was very guarded in his responses; he wouldn't elaborate on this question because . . . ." Or the interviewer might note that one particular question evoked a tremendously excited tone of voice, that he believed one particular point dwarfed all others in importance, or that the subject said one thing, but later implied that his actions contradicted his statement.

STEP #2:   **IS SOMETHING MISSING?** Senior executives should review responses for omissions and anomalies. There's no law that says you can't re-contact subjects for additional information. It may be that a question was poorly stated and has to be asked again. It's possible that the responses suggest another, more pertinent question, or a new line of inquiry. Get back on the phone.

STEP #3:   **DO WE NEED TO DO MORE?** It's always difficult to estimate in advance the number of calls that should be made. If no clear pattern emerges from the responses, or if there's an anomalous pattern, it may be wise to increase the number of calls. You may want to vary the type of people that you contact as well as the number of people.

STEP #4:   **SEPARATE SUPERIOR FROM SECONDARY NEEDS.** When looking over the collected data, keep your eye open for the superior need. It's not always easy to spot. You'll probably find many minor or isolated needs such as idiosyncratic customer complaints, a tiny segment of your market that has a wish that is impossible for you to fulfill cost-effectively, and half-hearted suggestions for new features. What you're looking for is a repeated, major theme—something that has the potential to impact your business dramatically. It may be a subtle shift in customer attitudes taking place in your industry, a technological development that is filtering into customer consciousness, or a refusal to accept any product that falls below a new, higher standard. Whatever it is, this need transcends all others. If you're the first to recognize and respond to it, you will satisfy your customer. And when customers are delighted, they reward sellers with repeat purchases and long-term loyalty.

If you follow the techniques described in this chapter, the superior need should emerge. Time and again, I've watched our clients' mouths drop in astonishment as they perused the data we collected and read through our evaluations. As soon as they came upon the superior need, they recognized they had discovered a key—a key that could unlock the marketplace.

When filtered through the steps described here, that formerly unintelligible customer voice becomes crystal clear. How to use that voice to identify superior needs in seven categories will be the focus of the following chapters.

Chapter 4

Delivery

"*Company X's quality is 90% of where I want it to be. It should be 100%. Company X has some communication problems with their inside personnel. Orders are early at times and late at times. They don't handle orders properly enough or carefully enough to avoid errors or avoid having the wrong order sent, for example . . . we want 100% on-time delivery.*"

In your quest to meet the superior need, you can start with any category. You may feel compelled to begin with the category where you're experiencing obvious difficulties. If everyone is screaming about your poor product quality and sales are plummeting, naturally that's where you'll focus your attention first.

If there is not an obvious problem area, start with delivery. It's the place where it's easiest to improve quickly. Unlike other categories, delivery contains a relatively small number of variables. Measures of success are also less ambiguous (as opposed to product quality, for instance, where there are all types of measures). I've seen organizations implement superior need delivery programs that have yielded dramatic results in just a few months.

Because a superior need strategy will be new to your organization, it's important to start off on the right foot. Delivery gives you the best chance of doing so by demonstrating the strategy's viability impressively and quickly. In addition, delivery is a good category to learn the language of the superior need, to become familiar with capturing the voice of the customer, and to understand how to interpret that voice and translate it into various tactics.

All this is not to say that finding and responding to the superior customer delivery need is easy. It's only "easy" if you use traditional customer satisfaction research methods. Then, you naturally assume that delivery equates to getting something somewhere on time. In most cases, it is not that simple.

SIX BASIC DELIVERY NEEDS

When you're searching for the superior delivery need, you usually have six areas to investigate. Though that might seem like a lot, it's far less than the number of possibilities in other categories. The key is to focus on the way customers prioritize these six needs and respond accordingly.

The Time Need. With all the talk about just-in-time delivery, you would think that this is the only thing that counts. There is not any question that it's important. Our perceptions of speed have changed radically in recent years. It used to be acceptable for a package to be delivered in a few days. Faster delivery services have changed all that, as have faxes, computers, and other technologies. In most instances, when customers specify a date for delivery. They want it on that date, give or take ten minutes.

The Spec Need. Customers expect 24 gauge steel and receive 22 gauge; they ordered a size 6 and receive a size 8. Delivering the wrong spec, even if it's only a little off, communicates a message of incompetence. Even if they accept the size 8 because the fit isn't bad and they don't want to deal with the return process, they won't forget this spec error. For most organizations, this is a delivery problem that's easy to rationalize and hard to fix.

The Quantity Need. You don't give the customer enough of what he ordered. It happens all the time for a number of reasons. For example, an 8 on the purchase order was misread as a 3, bad verbal miscommunication takes place, and a last-second change in the order occurs.

The Undamaged Need. You're responsible for a package moving through the system undamaged. Small nicks and scrapes say as much about your ability to fulfill that need as major damage. Even though you may be thousands of miles away from the ultimate customer destination, you will be held accountable for anything that goes wrong, even if it happens on the customer's loading dock.

The Location Need. It is not good enough just to "get it there." You have to deliver it precisely where the customer wants it. If you unload merchandise in the wrong place, you can cause major inconvenience to the customer's operation. Obviously, if you deliver it to the wrong house, department, or warehouse, you can expect a highly dissatisfied customer.

The Hassle-Free Need. Are your delivery people courteous, helpful, and informed? Or are they rude, apathetic, and ignorant? If a customer asks them about one of your products, can they answer convincingly and authoritatively? Companies often forget that the people who deliver their products are direct links with customers. How they look and act reflects on the company's delivery image. Even if they work for a common carrier, you need to ensure that they do their job properly. If they don't, look for another supplier.

THE UNARTICULATED NEED

Your customers may not directly communicate any of the previous six needs as the superior one. At least, they might not communicate it to your salespeople. It might lurk right below the surface, and your customer is unable or unwilling to articulate it.

If so, you have to identify it, and the techniques described in our chapter on the voice of the customer will help. Probe each of the six needs with questions, and you'll probably find what really will satisfy your customer and what will delight him.

One of our clients had received numerous complaints from customers about delivery errors. They couldn't figure out what they were doing wrong. All of their traditional research showed that they were scoring high for all delivery factors. We had them and their customers flow chart the delivery process. As we did, we discovered that they had been charting delivery based on the invoice slip and monitoring its progress as it was torn off and moved to the control room. We also learned that an informal protocol at many customer companies was writing changes and additions to the order on the back of the slip. Unfortunately, our client didn't always pay attention to what was on the back. As a result, "mistakes" were made that resulted in missing and wrong parts.

Another client, an electronics company, failed to visit one of its customers for 18 years. It didn't seem necessary since the customer never complained about anything, including the delivery process. Of course, this customer also gave a lot of work to suppliers other than my client. One day, a representative from the electronics company decided to go out and see the customer's facility. While he was there, he began talking with his customer contact who showed him how they received electronic components on the dock and then stored them in the warehouse. The rep noticed how long it was taking to complete the process, and he wondered out loud if it might be helpful if there were large labels identifying the component part on the box. (At the time, the package identification was a bar code, useful only to the inventory control manager.) After they put on the labels, the delivery time was cut by two-thirds.

The lessons learned:

♦ Flow chart the delivery process to spot the roadblocks and detours to customer needs.

♦ Visit customers regularly, observe the delivery process and question customers about what you observe.

TO MEET A SUPERIOR NEED, YOU MAY REQUIRE AN UNTRADITIONAL SOLUTION

Solutions to delivery problems tend to be traditional. If you're forced to speed up the delivery process, find a carrier who can do it faster. If you have to prevent damage to a product during shipping, use a stronger container.

But untraditional solutions are often required to meet a superior need. Here are four untraditional types of solutions you might consider:

1. **Capitalize on new technology.** Benetton, for instance, has all but done away with inventory. They've constructed a sophisticated, computerized tracking system that allows them to coordinate production and shipping with magical speed. As a

result, stores never have to wait for merchandise, and product doesn't gather dust in a warehouse.

Maybe a computerized system is your solution. Or perhaps it's as simple as a new piece of equipment. I was recently in a hobby shop with my son, looking for a present for his friend's birthday. We saw a model kit that seemed good, but my son wanted to look inside to determine if it was appropriate for his friend. Unfortunately, the box was covered in shrink wrap plastic. The salesman, however, told us to rip it off. When I started to protest, saying that I wasn't sure if I wanted to buy it and if I did, I didn't want to give a gift that looked "used," he showed me a machine the store had that re-shrink-wrapped any opened package. That machine made the delivery process delightful. It met my superior need.

2. **Take responsibility for the package after it leaves your hands.** Many companies assign a relatively arbitrary end point for their delivery responsibility. As soon as it's delivered to point A, it's someone else's job. But the customer doesn't always subscribe to that arbitrary cutoff point. For instance, you're at the supermarket about to pick your favorite box of cereal off the shelf when you notice that the package is ripped. You worry about tampering or spoilage, and you don't buy it. The store clerks have nicked the packages with their razor knives that they used to open the shipping containers. The cereal company can prevent this delivery problem by packing the cereal boxes in a carton with a Styrofoam inner slip that prevents damage. Yes, it's an additional expense; and yes, the store is at fault. But ultimately, it is the cereal company's customer, and they have the most to gain by preventing damage.

3. **Proactively notify customers of problems**. Typically, when shipments are delayed, we wait for customers to call and to complain about the delay. We're afraid to tell customers that we can't meet the due date. We should be more afraid, however, not to tell them. When we're silent, we violate the trust customers have placed in us. It's as if we purposely deceived them about the delivery date. Therefore, always notify them as soon as you suspect you're going to miss the deadline. Give them other options. Apologize. Try to pinpoint how long it will take before you can deliver.

4. **Facilitate "reverse delivery."** When you deliver the wrong or a damaged product, the return process can be a nightmare for customers. Too often, they have to go through a multi-step process that involves calling someone from your company on the phone, proving that the damage wasn't their fault, and repacking the damaged or wrong product. It is better if you inform your customers from the very start of the business relationship about how to go about reverse delivery. And if you make a mistake, compensate customers for the inconvenience. Give them a gift or a discount on the next delivery.

IT'S EASY TO MAKE MISTAKES

Delivery is the most human of processes; therefore, it's extraordinarily easy to make mistakes. From working with hundreds of companies over the years, I've culled some of the most flawed or ineffective solutions to delivery problems. Sometimes they occur because people aren't thinking. And sometimes, it's because people fail to discern the customer's superior need. Beware of the following:

Following one mistake with another. At some point, you're going to mess up a delivery. Customers will forgive you as long as you don't make a habit of it. However, what they won't forgive is compounding the initial mistake with another one. One way of compounding the mistake is to leave the wrong product on the customer' dock for days (or weeks) until you can get someone to pick it up. If your customer's superior need is a supplier who is prompt, this will demonstrate that you can't meet that need. The wrong shipment sitting on the dock is highly visible testimony to that inability. Everyone should have a plan in place that ensures fast, efficient responses to delivery errors.

Borrowing other people's solutions. Some organizations believe that customer needs are interchangeable; that if they borrow what worked for Company A, it will work for Company B. For instance, a company tries to duplicate a delivery method used by another one of its plants or in another one of its regions. They have irrefutable proof that it is effective, so they copy it. I've found that delivery solutions need to be tailored to specific situations and environments. While a common carrier may work great in Region A, it may be ill-suited to Region B.

Spending too much or too little money. When delivery problems crop up, some organizations throw money at the problems. They hire more people, buy more trucks, switch to faster, more expensive planes from slower, less expensive trains. But they never address the superior need; namely, substituting money for knowledge of that need. The other extreme is failing to spend enough money to meet a customer need. The philosophy is, "It's just a minor delivery problem." These people consider things such as pricing, product quality and company image to be far more important than the less glamorous delivery issues. Though delivery isn't glamorous, it can make or break a customer relationship.

Ignoring the customer's need between purchase and use of the product. A delivery job isn't finished once the customer hands over the money. Yet, how many times have you gone into a store and have been ignored by the sales clerk after you've made the purchase; how long have you had to wait before the package was put into your hands; how many times has the sales clerk acted resentful because you asked to have your package gift wrapped? Organizations ignore both their consumer and industrial customers during this interim period. This is a shame, since you may have done a great delivery job until that point, and it's all gone for naught.

WHAT WILL DELIGHT YOUR CUSTOMER?

Answer this question and you'll likely answer your customer's superior need. Would he or she be delighted not if you met the deadline, but if you consistently delivered the goods two days before it? Would your customer call you up and praise you if you could go an entire year with less than 1% of your deliveries out of spec?

Do everything possible to discover what will thrill your customers. Because delivery is a relatively cut-and-dried process, you don't have to be a rocket scientist to unearth the key need. It's simply a matter of formulating a series of questions around each of the six need classifications previously discussed. When your customer's voice gets excited, when he says, "If anyone could guarantee us that kind of delivery, we'd pay anything," then you'll know that you've hit *the* need.

Chapter 5

Pricing

"We measure price to value in terms of yield, rejection loss, on-time delivery, and metallurgic review. Company Z thinks their galvanized material is worth more than any other supplier's but they think that way because they are trying to make a profit on their latest technological investment. They are not fooling anyone on pricing."

If you can meet a superior customer need, you can name your price and get it. Of course, the step from point A to point B isn't as easy as it sounds. The obstacles are many. You may be relying on the traditional cost-plus pricing formula that automatically places the superior need on the back burner. Or you may be unable or unwilling to identify that need. Or you may decide (wrongly) that your customer has no superior need. Or you may ignore customer need and price your product or service so that you're the lowest bidder or according to what the market will bear.

Whatever the obstacle, it's difficult to get around it. How do you ignore traditional pricing formulas or quarterly earnings pressures? This is why customers complain so bitterly about prices. Both industrial and consumer customers frequently feel products are unfairly priced; that the mark-up is sky-high and the quality doesn't justify the mark-up.

According to our extensive database, very few American companies are performing in the upper quartile of customer satisfaction, yet, they're pricing their products and services as if they are indeed in the upper quartile.

The solution isn't lower prices; it's improved customer satisfaction. Satisfied customers not only are willing to pay premium prices, but they're also glad to do so. Imagine, for a moment, that you could pack so much value into your product or service that customers are willing to pay virtually anything. If you think you've died and gone to pricing heaven, let's focus on a strategy that can have you singing with the angels.

TANGIBLES AND INTANGIBLES

When it comes to pricing policies, organizations spend too much time on the tangible aspects of a product and very little time on the intangible elements. Tangibles are such things as the number and type of product features, the quality of materials, the breakthrough technology behind a particular product benefit, and so forth. Typically, companies look at these tangibles and determine if they justify a given when price is compared to other products in the category.

There's no question; tangibles are important. But the superior need can also be found in the intangibles. They're the invisible things that support and cement customer relationships. They can range from the image projected by advertising to customer services to delivery time frames. Let me give you an example of how intangibles relate to pricing. When your domestic car breaks down, you call the dealer and he says, "Bring it in." The response is different at certain import car dealers. Their cars don't have any more tangible advantages than the domestics. Yet, they have plenty of intangibles. When you call up and say your car has broken down, the service manager replies, "Thanks for calling. We'll have a tow truck sent out to you right away, he should be arriving in 20 minutes, and we'll have a courtesy car for you that will get there a few minutes after that." When his car is returned after being fixed, it has been washed and cleaned, and a note of apology for any inconvenience is on the front seat.

A lot of people will pay many more dollars for an imported car than for a domestic one because of these intangibles. The superior need is for a dealer who turns the odious task of car repair into a quick, convenient, and courteous process.

If you haven't paid much attention to the intangibles, here's an exercise to help you.

The following is a list of intangible-related statements that may or may not apply to your company's products. Place a check mark next to the statements that you think customers might naturally come up with when they're thinking about your company's brands:

___1. "They feel like they're built to last forever."

___2. "They make everything so easy."

___3. "It's a status symbol, no question about it."

___4. "I feel like I can trust it."

___5. "It's more convenient than others."

___6. "I feel like they made it with me in mind."

___7. "I can't imagine buying another brand."

___8. "Their people (customer contacts) really enjoy what they're doing, and it shows."

If you can get customers to say one or more of the above about your products—or a similar phrase that expresses their gratitude for your meeting a superior need—then your price is never too high. Certain brands have done a terrific job of providing customers with intangibles (e.g., Morton, Motorola, Bridgestone/Firestone, DuPont, Exxon, FMC, General Electric, B. F. Goodrich, Honeywell, Navistar, and Pepsi). They could place checks next to at least one and probably a majority of the eight quotes above.

If you cannot do the same, the problem might have to do with miscommunication between your organization and the customer. If your mindset is A and your customer's mindset is B, then you're never going to find a happy pricing medium.

PRICE AND RELATIONSHIPS

What happens to pricing when a company and its customers are operating on different wavelengths? A business-to-business story spotlights the problem.

One of the country's leading package goods manufacturers got caught up in the quality movement and, as part of its new quality program, told vendors that they expected them to become "partners" with the company. They would become partners in the sense that there would be no more of the adversarial buy-sell relationship that formerly existed. Instead, the company would help vendors move up the quality learning curve, and vendors would realize an estimated 25% cost savings through process improvements and reduced rework. The company suggested that they and their vendors share in those savings. Because the company would be responsible for what vendors will save, they should get a cut.

The vendors responded positively. Guarantees of long-term contracts and volume made the "partnership" proposal from the company palatable. So they agreed to the concept. What they didn't agree to, and what they didn't expect, was that the company's purchasing agent would continue to give contracts to the lowest bidder!

The vendors were confused. This was not part of the new quality program. It violated the spirit of their agreement with the company. Lowest bidders were supposed to be a thing of the past. It turned out that the company thought so too—at least upper management did. But they had neglected to communicate the new quality order to the purchasing agents who were blithely following tradition because their performance reviews and compensation evaluations had not been adjusted to reflect management's newly articulated objectives.

Though this is a business-to-business example, the principle applies in the consumer arena as well. When a relationship between customer and company is violated, the fragile, shared assumptions about price crumple. Here are the three deadly sins of pricing that have destroyed more than one customer relationship:

1. **Reducing Quality.** An organization decides that it can substitute a lower-cost, lower-quality part or material in a product without the customer caring or even knowing. The goal, of course, is to increase margins. Whether it's substituting an inferior type of chocolate in a candy bar or replacing a metal part with a plastic one, the company-customer relationship suffers. Consequently, customers begin to feel overcharged when they purchase the product.

2. **Raising Prices Without a Good Reason.** The key words are "good reason." Organizations often feel that they're fully justified in raising prices, either because competitors are doing so or because they're passing on increased costs to customers. Yet, they

violate customer relationships when they don't communicate these reasons or, more often, customers don't feel the reasons justify increases. Oil companies, airlines, and automobile dealers are three industries guilty of this practice. When the reason for the increase has nothing to do with the superior need of the customer, the increase is a relationship violation.

3. **Playing Games With Prices.** Playing the trade dealing game with retailers can have dangerous repercussions. Your product is discounted so much and so often that customers begin to distrust your pricing policies or expect the slashed price to be the rule rather than the exception. Ultimately, you're going to have to go back to selling at a nondiscounted price; and when that time comes, your customer may feel that you haven't been playing fairly.

FORMING PARTNERSHIPS

The ideal relationship between customer and company is a partnership. In partnerships, both parties feel that they're getting something for something. The relationship is supportive rather than adversarial. In partnerships, prices are always considered fair. The seller and buyer have worked out an agreement where a reasonable amount of money is exchanged for a reasonable value.

How are partnerships with customers formed? By the following three golden rules:

1. **Establishing Two-Way Communication**—creating a continuous dialog between seller and buyer. This can involve anything from in-bound communication efforts, such as a customer service hotline to focus groups, and other forms of research and

outbound communication initiatives, including customer newsletters, user groups, and trade shows.

2. **Building a Bond of Trust**—never doing anything that can be perceived as deceitful or underhanded or that would make a customer feel betrayed (e.g., failing to inform the public about even a minor defect in a product).

3. **Adding Value**—looking for ways to meet the superior need is another way of phrasing this point. (How to do so will be discussed in the next section.)

A partnership has numerous touchpoints; that is, key interactions between customer and company. Those consumer touchpoints include ads, articles, sales promotions and presentations, direct mail, speeches, service calls, and phone contacts. Industrial touchpoints include one-on-one meetings (i.e., between purchasing agent and vendor), engineering evaluation of prospective product, one top executive meeting with another, and so forth.

Through these touchpoints, the partnership is strengthened or weakened. Too often, the partnership is weakened because the seller fails to communicate the value that he's providing to the customer. It is not enough to provide value—you have to make the customer aware of the value that you're providing. It is not enough for Motorola to win a Baldridge Award; they need to use advertising and other communication tools to explain how that award translates into customer value. If this isn't done, price will become a problem.

I know of a very successful business-to-business packaging company. The company charges more than many of its competitors, but they feel their prices are justified since not only is their packaging of superior quality, but they also provide tremendous support for their customers. For instance, this packaging company estimates that they spend 8,000 hours annually on field engineering to ensure that their package works properly and to assist customers with line process problems.

One day, a customer's purchasing agent complained about the company's pricing, saying that in terms of dollars per thousand, it was higher than the competition. For the first time, the company representative detailed the product support commitment, explaining how that support translated into greater efficiency. Unconvinced, the purchasing agent responded that they could probably put one of their junior engineers in the plant and get the same efficiency for less cost, to which the sales rep responded, "We are intimately involved in our customers' 400 plants and bring you improvements and suggestions that are a result of that accumulated experience. Your junior engineer doesn't have access to all those other plants, and his recommendations are necessarily limited."

Finally, the purchasing agent understood the value that was added into the company's price, and for the first time the agent realized that the price was justified.

The moral: never assume the customer understands the value that you add. Always take the time to explain it in clear, concise terms.

SUPERIOR NEEDS, SUPERIOR PRICING STRATEGIES

If you can unearth a current or prospective customer's superior need, you don't have to be concerned about charging too few or too many pennies or even dollars. Contrary to what you may have been taught, price becomes a secondary issue in a purchasing decision when a product or service meets the highest of all needs.

The trick of finding that need is related to discomfort. This is called Subjective Units of Discomfort (SUDS), which is a wonderful term that I recently encountered at a seminar. If you can create a product (or an image) that reduces a customer's SUDS level or that increases his or her comfort level, then you're well on your way to winning the price war. What makes people comfortable or uncomfortable? Though there are a number of factors, let's look at the five most common ones and how you can turn them into a price advantage.

1. **FLEXIBILITY.** Some products and services are inflexible; they can only be used in certain ways at certain times. For years, supermarkets were closed late at night. Then, convenience stores increased the flexibility of the hours, and they were able to charge significantly more for their merchandise. Products, too, can be inflexible. For instance, a European company recognized that vacuum cleaners were quite loud and couldn't be used at certain times (e.g., when children are napping, when someone is trying to concentrate, when people are trying to

watch television or listen to music). Therefore, they created a vacuum cleaner with a microprocessor chip and black box that monitors the decibel level of the motor, reverses the decibel mix, and creates a sound in counterpoint to the noise that neutralizes the sound. In other words, they created a virtually noiseless vacuum. Though this very basic technology adds a few dollars to the manufacturing process, the European company is charging a few hundred dollars more and getting it. Why? Because it gives the customer a great deal more time and flexibility to vacuum.

2. **THE HUMAN FACTOR.** If you've ever bought a product or have been provided with a service that seemed better designed for a machine than for a person, then you understand this comfort category. Tools that are difficult to grip, banks that treat you like dirt, lawnmowers that are hard to start, and toys created for children that confound even adults are only a few examples. The list of inhuman products and services is endless. No matter what price you pay for them, you feel that you're being overcharged.

I know of a company that recently humanized the alarm clock. For years, people have looked upon the alarm clock as a necessary evil. Alarms have always been grating, regardless of sound type. The alternative of a music alarm has proven ineffective because people fall back asleep to the music. Therefore, this company created an alarm that starts at a low, barely audible level and rises gradually in volume. Before it reaches an obnoxious, piercing level, you've been awakened gently and given adequate warning to get up and get out of bed. Needless to say, this alarm clock costs more than others, but the lower discomfort level makes any price seem worth it.

3. **CONSCIENCE.** We don't have to look any further than the growing popularity of environmentally safe products to grasp this particular comfort category. People are willing to pay a bit more for a product that's biodegradable. Even if that product doesn't look as attractive (e.g., brown coffee filters) or isn't as convenient (e.g., bottles you have to recycle rather than throw in the garbage), people are willing to pay more for them. Beyond the environment, conscience price-raising tactics can include substituting natural food ingredients for artificial ones (you feel better serving it to yourself and others), advertising politically correct stances (honoring a group's or country's boycott or supporting their cause) and America-first sloganeering (American automobile companies).

4. **SHAPES AND SIZES.** By changing the shape or size of a product, you can change the customer's comfort level. In electronics, computers, tape players, televisions, video cameras, and many other devices have all become more attractive as they were downsized. Carrying a bulky tape player around to listen to cassettes was literally uncomfortable; a Walkman™ was the definition of comfort. Morton Salt, in one simple but dramatic downsizing, created smaller blocks of salt (for water softeners) that could be lifted by ordinary human beings into car trunks. Vitamins in the shapes of animals and cartoon characters have become extremely popular with kids who for some reason feel more comfortable eating things they know than things they don't. In clothing, oversized sweaters and sweatshirts have become trendy. Changing sizes and shapes are some of the easiest and most cost-efficient ways that organizations can add value to customers and dollars to their bottom lines.

5. **AURAS.** Sometimes the superior need is for distinctiveness. You're tired of the same old product (especially the same old parity product). You want something different, something with pizazz, and something with which you can identify. You feel uncomfortable with a product that seems stamped out of the cookie cutter. Packaging, promotion, advertising, public relations, and other marketing tools can surround an otherwise undistinguished product with an aura. Consider how the cartoon character Rusty Jones turned an ordinary undercoating from a $1.1 million business into a $150 million one. Designer labels, exquisitely sculpted perfume bottles, and a trustworthy product spokesperson can confer an aura that will allow you to get a better price.

THE RULES COME SECOND

I'm not suggesting that you dismiss your pricing strategy. Certainly, you have to factor in your various costs, competitors' prices, and profit margins. But these aren't the only or the first things that you should consider.

No matter what kind of product or service you have—new, improved, old, parity, niche, and so forth— you're facing more competition than ever before. Unless you're in the upper echelon of customer satisfaction (as mentioned earlier, the odds are you're not), you can't routinely pass on cost increases to customers or assume your brand name automatically guarantees brand loyalty. Unless our government takes an extreme protectionist stance, you're also not going to be able to compete on price alone with many foreign companies.

Therefore, before setting a price, do the following:

♦ Avoid the three deadly sins of pricing.

♦ Consider both the tangible and intangible as
pects of your product or service.

♦ Form a partnership with customers.

♦ Find the superior need via comfort levels.

If you've done all this, your price should be at or
near the top of the category. Then, and only then, can
you look at your price from the perspective of traditional pricing formulas.

There's a story that exemplifies this point. I know
a guy who writes aphorisms on postcards and sells
them for a quarter. He did fairly well. The sayings
were funny and philosophical. But then others started
to steal his sayings, using them for their own commer-
cial purposes. He filed suit against them, maintaining
they were violating his copyright. During the legal
process, his lawyer told him that it was important for
him to have a series of rules and procedures that
governed his aphorisms. These rules and procedures
would make his case stronger.

So the creator of these sayings looked over the
hundreds of postcards he'd written and wrote down
a set of rules based on what existed. For instance, no
aphorism was longer than 16 words, so Rule #1 was
that they could not contain more than 17 words. He
discovered that his aphorisms all ended with an unexpected twist, so unexpected twists were Rule #2. In this
manner, he produced a series of rules after the fact.
(He also won his court case.)

Take the same backward approach to pricing
rules. After you've found the superior need and have
incorporated it, then make sure that the price you
instinctively think you should charge is in line with
your profit requirements. When you put the rules first,
the superior need appears irrelevant. You've already
figured out the price, so why waste time on anything
else? But when you leave the price open, you're free
to take the steps that will add value to your product

and that will tap into your customers' superior needs. The price you ultimately choose evolves naturally from this process, and customers will feel that the price you charge reflects genuine rather than artificial value.

Chapter 6

Product Quality

"*The definition of quality is expanding. In the old days, quality was just how quickly manufacturers could get their machinery to run, how well they could adapt to running on our line—the speed and efficiency. . . . All of that is changing. . . . Quality used to be just one small aspect of serving our needs within the manufacturing end, but also had to represent the final consumer through packaging that didn't leak, appealing graphics. . . . The new definition of quality has to take into account the voice of the customer as well as warehousing, manufacturing and needs within the channel.*"

Product quality doesn't begin in the factory; it only ends there.

Many quality gurus have failed to recognize this fact. In their quest for quality, they've advocated radical changes in the manufacturing process designed to reduce defects, increase reliability and durability, and so forth. If only it were so simple. If only we could wave a wand over the assembly line and produce the magical quality we so desperately seek.

Quality is achieved by seeking out and meeting the superior customer need. That's where it starts, and everything else flows from it. If you want to build a quality mousetrap, find out what features customers desperately desire. Do not ignore the customers and go straight to your manufacturing people and say, "We've got to build a better mousetrap." The world will not beat a path to your door.

The superior need may be a mousetrap that isn't potentially harmful to children; or one that operates silently; or one that doesn't hurt those cute little furry creatures; or one with a 99% catch rate. Find that superior need (or needs) and design your product around it. That's when you'll earn your quality stripes. How do you do it? Follow these seven steps:

STEP 1: FREE YOURSELF FROM OLD QUALITY DEFINITIONS

Quality definitions change quickly. Superior customer needs emerge, catalyzed by raised expectations, media hype, changing environments, and many other factors. Definitions change for every type of product.

Think about the cars, computers, televisions, food, clothes, or anything else you bought five years ago. The odds are that they no longer meet your highest-quality specifications. The car doesn't have an airbag; your winter coat is missing a new, more effective thermal insulator; your frozen food dinner isn't microwaveable; your computer printer isn't laser.

Despite the alacrity with which these quality definitions change, many of us fail to let go of the old definitions. We refuse to discern or accept our customers' new definitions of quality. Why? Because the old definitions are comfortable. It's scary to think about a superior customer need—one that will soon make a major product line obsolete.

Is your organization a victim of its old definitions? Take the following self-examination:

DEFINITION CHANGE INVENTORY

Begin by identifying a major product category with which your company has been involved for at least ten years. Write the name of that category on a piece of paper.

Next, write the industry definition of quality for that category ten years ago. Include all the standard measures—speed, reliability, durability, and so forth.

Now, write the industry definition five years ago.

Finally, write the industry definition today.

Take another piece of paper and divide it in half. On the left-hand side, write down all the areas where your company was quickly aware of the changing definition and responded effectively. On the right-hand side, note all the areas where your company failed to do so.

The best way to avoid the trap of old definitions is to redefine "quality" for your organization regularly. Whenever you receive a critical piece of information suggesting a superior customer need—from research, from the media, and complaints from customers—rewrite your definition. Spread the new definition throughout your organization and empower everyone to act upon it. It may mean dramatic changes in manufacturing, R&D, marketing, and operations. So be it. It's better to make changes based on new definitions than to be operating under false assumptions fostered by old definitions.

STEP 2: REDEFINE QUALITY VIA FRESH PERSPECTIVES

Sometimes, our experience is a curse rather than a blessing. Veterans of companies have looked at a product the same way for so long that they have difficulty viewing the product from a fresh perspective. But we need to view our products differently. If you saw the movie, "The Dead Poets Society," you'll understand what I mean. In the film, the teacher encouraged his pupils to jump up and stand on their desks. The goal was to free them from their traditional, desk-bound, seated positions and to allow them an alternative way of looking at their academic subjects. When students gained a new perspective, truths about art would emerge.

Similarly, superior customer needs emerge when organizations gain fresh perspectives on their products. We have a client in the specialty chemicals business. For years, a coating chemical has included a significant percentage of silicone. Silicone is used because of its "forgiving" properties; it can take a nick and bounce back. The quality definition in chemical coatings, therefore, has always included silicone.

On behalf of our client, we surveyed customers to determine how they defined quality. Based on our research, we found the glimmering of a superior need: even better performance at a lower cost.

We met with our client and shared our findings. The technical people in the meeting all responded that the silicone base sets parameters on both cost and performance. But we kept probing. We asked our client if there was any way to get to a higher level, to come closer to the customer definition.

Then a young engineer spoke. He hadn't been with the company long; he came from a different industry background than most of the people in the room. He said, "You know, we can do the same thing with a polymer, rather than with silicone."

There was dead silence. Then everyone began asking the young engineer questions. It turned out that silicone had been introduced into the product category years ago when polymers were little used or understood. No one in the company was familiar with polymer technology. No one, that is, except the young engineer, who had a great deal of experience manipulating polymers.

He led the company's effort to develop a new, polymer-based product with only a trace of silicone, included for comfort purposes (customers expected coatings to have silicone, and it would have required an expensive education campaign to convince them otherwise). Using the polymer, the company developed a product at a fraction of the former cost (silicone was very expensive) and with greatly improved performance. They took the market by storm.

The point is that fresh perspectives can redefine quality and find more efficient and effective alternative ways of meeting superior customer needs.

How do you find fresh perspectives to redefine quality? Here are some helpful approaches:

Bring in fresh faces. Like our client company, find someone with a different background than most of the people who usually discuss quality issues. Perhaps it's someone who just joined the firm, an outside consultant, or somebody from a different group who usually doesn't attend the meetings.

Encourage alternative viewpoints. Sometimes, people are afraid to redefine quality. They're afraid that they'll be laughed at or censured because of their "challenging" viewpoint. Therefore, key quality people must feel empowered to stand the definition on its head. One technique might be to have a meeting in which people are forced to redefine quality. Even if they feel the definition is wrong, they must offer a redefinition for discussion. Out of that discussion might come some viable new thinking about quality.

Listen long and hard to the voice of the customer. Use the techniques suggested in the previous chapter to get at real customer perceptions of quality. All that closed-ended research you've been relying on for years may be misleading. A probing, insightful discussion with your customers might reveal that quality isn't what you thought at all—it's what they (the customers) think.

STEP 3: SEARCH FOR THE HIDDEN NEED

Superior customer needs often exist just below the surface. Standard research won't unearth them. Customers may not even realize what they are themselves unless they're pushed. But if you can "push" effectively, you may find a way to improve product quality dramatically.

BMW has obviously done this. In their ads, they promote their new air-cleaning system that removes 97% of dust and other particles from the interior.

In the past, the air inside the car was not part of the quality equation. It was assumed that customers didn't hold manufacturers responsible for pollution caused by sources unrelated to BMW. After all, what could BMW do about other vehicles' exhaust fumes that permeated the interior when their drivers were sitting in traffic?

It turns out that they could do plenty. Though I'm not sure how BMW learned that this was a concern of its customers, I assume they did some top-notch research and were surprised to find that interior air purity was integral to customers' definitions of quality. It might not be something that people would list as their top priority or immediately mention in response to a question about car quality, but it is something that's hidden just below the surface.

I've found that virtually every product category has at least one of these hidden needs. Sometimes, it is obscured by more obvious needs. For instance, television manufacturers have invested heavily in big-screen television technology based on customer demand for larger screens. I suspect, however, that if open-ended, well-designed research were conducted, it would reveal that big-screen televisions mask a superior, hidden need. The typical customer might say, "Sure, I'd like a bigger screen television. But you know what I really want? I want to recreate the movie theater experience in my own house." I'd like to see a portable screen as big as my rec room wall, or at least one that would get a movie image in the right dimensions, and I'd like a button that would control the focus definition, kind of the way you control it when you decide where you'll sit in the theater."

The hidden need for this customer is recreating the movie theater experience, not just a bigger screen. For him, quality is the former and not the latter. Finding the hidden need can be facilitated by using the following interview techniques with customers:

Ask "What if" questions. Don't be satisfied with a customer's definition of quality. Ask such things as: "What if we could make a television ten times bigger than the one you currently own? Would you want it?" Or, "What if such a television was available? How much more would you be willing to pay for it?"

Remove reality-imposed restrictions. Customers don't voice their hidden needs because they don't believe they're realistic; they don't think what they want is possible. Remove those limitations by saying, "Assume for a second we could make a television screen as big as your rec room wall. If we could do that, would you be interested in buying one?"

Give the customer a blank canvas. Too often, researchers ask interview subjects to connect the dots. By the way their questions are framed, researchers guide people along a path. Yes or no and multiple-choice questions are often the culprits. Hidden needs emerge when customers are allowed to fantasize and to talk spontaneously. For instance, "Tell me, if you could have any television you wanted in your home, and if you didn't have to worry about price or technological constraints, what kind of television would you have?"

STEP 4: ASK: SAYS WHO?

"We need to reduce our defects per part by X%."

"We need to increase the life of part Y."

"Your product isn't as good as Company B's product because it only lasts two years."

"I'd be more inclined to purchase your product if it got the job done faster."

To all of these quality-imperative statements, I would reply, "*Says who?*"

It's such a simple question, yet it's one that many organizations fail to ask before embarking on expensive and often futile quality quests.

Who says? If it's the CEO or other top executive, why are they saying it? On what are they basing their decisions about quality? An industry study? A report in the trade press? Advice from a consultant?

If it's the customer, what customer is it? In other words, if you've conducted a market research study among customers, are those surveyed your primary audience? Are they decision makers? Decision influencers? Or, are they people twice removed from the decision-making process?

Answering the "says who" question enables you to differentiate the superior need from the secondary need.

For instance, you're an executive with a power tool company and become alarmed when a survey shows that 48 percent of respondents require a drill that lasts 3,000 hours. Your company's drill is designed to last 500 hours. If you fail to ask, says who, you may embark on a very expensive crusade to redesign your drill. But if you ask says who, you may find that of the 48 percent of respondents who want a longer-lasting drill, 95 percent are small, entrepreneurial construction firms. Your primary market is large construction firms. When you look at your survey more closely (or when you conduct a new, better survey), you find that your market requires a drill to last only 300 hours—the average amount of use for one construction job. You learn that most large construction companies consider these drills to be "throwaways." They usually disappear on the job site (theft or other shrinkage problems give them this short life span).

Therefore, it makes no sense to create a drill that lasts 3,000 hours, unless you plan to target a different market.

One of the biggest "says who" mistakes organizations make is: taking early adopters' words as gospel.

"Early adopters" are those people who like to be on the leading edge of trends. They want to be the first on their blocks to have the newest technological gimmick or the first company in the industry to use the latest high-tech material.

If you base your organization's quality program on what early adopters say, you could be in a lot of trouble. Their definition of the superior need is often far ahead of the definition of non-early adopters. Every year, companies bring out products that are ahead of their time: laser disc players, "green" (environmentally conscious) products, gimmick-laden automobiles, and many, many others. In some instances, these companies' efforts were catalyzed by early adopters and their wildly enthusiastic response to the new product in test or based on research. In short, they created high-quality products for a larger marketplace that wasn't ready for them. It doesn't mean that they'll never be ready for them. When first introduced, light beer failed miserably. Store bar codes were supposed to arrive in 1965, but it took many more years until retailers accepted them.

To avoid these problems, when you receive input related to product quality, ask the following "Says Who" questions:

1. **Who is the source of your information?** Can you check out its reliability (i.e., who conducted the study, how was it conducted, was it done with 10 people or 1,000?)

2. **Is the source credible?** Is it a combination of open-ended and closed-ended research (good) or only closed-ended (bad)?

3. **Is the source your primary market?** Is it decision makers in that market; is it decision influencers; is it far removed from the decision-making process?

4. **Is the source early adopters?** If so, take the information with more than a few grains of salt.

STEP 5: LOOK FOR AND CONTROL THE QUALITY ISSUES THAT HAVE ALWAYS BEEN "NOT YOUR RESPONSIBILITY"

Organizations narrowly define quality: it's only the product itself. Anything "outside" of the product is beyond the manufacturer's control. Such narrow definitions can dramatically lower customer perceptions of product quality. When companies fail to take responsibility for outside factors that affect quality, they might as well insert defective parts into their products. The results are the same: the products don't perform up to specifications. Here are a few examples:

A customer pays $500 for a television, but the television manufacturer does not accept responsibility for a terrible picture caused by a poorly placed antenna or improper cable hookup.

A customer pays $2,000 for a computer, but the computer company says that it is not their fault that the computer was wiped out by a power surge, and that the customer failed to protect himself against that possibility.

A customer pays $400 for a plane ticket, and the flight is terrible. A storm causes a three-hour delay, and when the plane is in the air, the turbulence makes the flight miserable. The airline, however, says there's nothing it can do about the weather.

In each of these instances, an organization has defined quality narrowly for its own benefit, not for the customer's.

In the first two instances, it would have been relatively easy for the organizations to expand their definitions of quality. The television manufacturer could have made it their business to ensure the antenna or cable service was installed properly; they could have provided a service representative to help with installation or an emergency assistance number for customers to call if there was a problem with installation. The computer company could have provided their customers with a product to protect against power surges. The additional cost could have been easily absorbed.

The airline situation is a bit more problematic, but no less solvable. True, they can't control the weather. However, they shouldn't act as if it's a big shock or unusual circumstance when weather problems create "quality" problems. At the very least, they should provide customers with meaningful compensation for weather-caused flight delays. (Meaningful means more than a free drink on the flight—perhaps half-off coupons for a flight to the same destination.) They might also devote a significant amount of money to develop devices that eliminate or minimize the effects of turbulence. Rather than accepting turbulent flights as an unfortunate reality, airlines should invest more money in finding a solution to the problem. Cruise lines wouldn't be as successful as they have been if they hadn't developed ship-stabilizing technology and helped to fund research for sea sickness drugs. Imagine an airline that could advertise: "We guarantee you no turbulence on our flights or your money back!"

What quality issues has your organization ignored because you've always held they're outside your control? Look for those issues and develop ways to bring them under control. The superior need can exist outside traditional definitions.

STEP 6: DON'T ASK THE CUSTOMER IF THE SPECS ARE RIGHT

This is an easy quality mistake to make. You have your specifications in hand, and you go to your business-to-business customer and say, "Are these right?"

You might do the same thing on a consumer level via market research. Your market research firm approaches customers with questions such as, "Yes or no, would you buy a product that delivers Benefits A, B, and C?"

Customers routinely confirm specs you give them. Why not? It doesn't require a lot of thought, and it's easy to do. It's not that they're lying to you. They're just not giving the issue much thought.

That's your fault. You're leading them to an answer. You're not getting them emotionally involved in the issues.

The solution is simple: Let them define the specs. Ask open-ended questions about their quality requirements. Let them furnish the definitions without the straitjacket of leading questions and "yes-or-no" answers.

STEP 7: SPEND MORE TIME WITH CUSTOMERS

How much time does the average executive in your organization spend with customers, either in person or on the phone? Conduct your own survey. Take a sampling of 20 executives from different groups and divisions, and ask them to note their customer interactions over the past month. Specifically, ask them to tell you

♦ The length of each interaction.

♦ The mode of the interaction (phone, mail, computer, in-person).

♦ What was discussed during the interaction.

I think you'll be shocked to find that customer interaction is rare outside the sales group. Even when there is interaction, it is shocking to discover that product quality issues are rarely addressed.

Here's a recommendation that will shock you further. Companies should insist that all their people spend one-third of their time with customers. "They won't have the time to get anything done." That's the usual protest to this recommendation. My response: there isn't anything worth doing if your people are light-years removed from the customer.

Research and development, product design, and manufacturing can only do so much to make up the gap between a company and its customers. These groups all may be very skilled and state-of-the-art, but they may be applying their skills based on a false premise. They may assume the customer's definition of quality is something far different than it actually is.

Therefore, everyone should be encouraged to talk with and listen to the customer at every opportunity. Don't depend solely on market research—no matter how good the research. Combine it with your people's experiences.

Here are some suggestions on how to gain these experiences:

Encourage everyone to spend some time each month in the trenches by working the customer assistance phone lines in the store, by going out with salespeople for customer meetings, by sitting in on focus groups. (McDonald's is one company that does this; its top executives sling burgers so they don't lose touch with their customers).

Review written correspondence from customers. Every organization receives thousands of letters from customers. Too often, top executives treat this correspondence like movie stars treat fan letters. Everyone in an organization should pay attention to these letters, especially those who focus on product quality issues. They should look for common themes of praise or criticism.

Seize every opportunity to ask: What do you think of this product? If you're like most people, you pass up numerous opportunities to ask other people what they think of your company's products. You see someone looking at your product in the store or putting it in the shopping basket, you see the product in the home of a friend, and you hear a retail salesperson talking about the product. Talk to these people. It won't be scientific research, and that's the point. You'll receive highly subjective responses about your product. They're valuable when you hear a repeated theme, such as "This is the worst piece of junk I've ever seen," or "The company could double the price and I'd still buy it."

QUALITY THEORIES AND QUALITY REALITIES

There are a lot of theories floating around relating to quality. There's nothing wrong with most of them. In fact, there's a lot right with some of them. Crosby, especially, has pioneered an approach that is humanistic and personalized, providing an effective structure for total quality management. But even Crosby occasionally fails to emphasize the voice of the customer within the quality equation as early and as often as is necessary.

If Crosby is a visionary who sometimes takes his eye off the customer, his cronies in quality have more serious problems.

Deming tends to be a bit myopic, especially when it comes to his precious statistics. His approach favors numbers over people, placing a premium on zero defects and creating an environment that can fail to factor in the needs of internal and external customers.

Juran focuses on current processes and doesn't look into the future at emerging customer needs. His cross-functional teams may be great at producing a product faster and more efficiently than anyone else, but they sometimes don't recognize that the product they've created no longer meets the customer's need.

Quality experts can debate the merits and demerits of Crosby, Deming and Juran, but one thing they should agree on: none of them prioritizes the superior customer need.

The seven steps discussed in this chapter are designed to do exactly that.

Find that superior need and meet it with your product. After you do that, the customer will be forgiving. He'll forgive a product that's overpriced, that's unattractively packaged, and that has poor retail distribution. A product that meets a need that the customer has prayed and hoped and wished that someone would meet is worth its weight in Baldrige points. Meeting this need can overcome many other liabilities. It can give a product the rare quality stamp of approval.

Chapter 7

Emergencies

"An emergency arises when it becomes critical for some reason to get products which had been ordered but not yet received about one week to one month ahead of the originally scheduled delivery date. . . . Lately, it seems that we have had the critical need once or twice a week. When this comes up we have to call Company Q 15 or 20 times and then contact someone higher up before we can get things moving. . . . Company Q could be excellent if we could get a response with one or two phone calls and less effort on our part about 95% of the time. Presently this occurs less than 10% of the time."

B efore I discuss this customer satisfaction component, I had better define my terms. Specifically, I
should distinguish between "emergencies" and "crises." The crises are few and far between for most
organizations. Crises are such things as a product
tampering incident or an environmentally related ca-
tastrophe. Emergencies, on the other hand, are nothing more than problems that threaten to spin out of
control such as product shortages, missed deadlines,
defects, and so forth. In some instances, the customer
is never aware of the emergency. A computer crashes
and loses crucial information that creates shipping
delays. Organizations rarely let their consumer customers know that an emergency occurred or is occur-
ring. General Motors doesn't tell the world that a new
model will be late for shipping because of a design
flaw that it recently discovered. Industrial customers

generally are aware of the problems caused by emergencies, but they're kept in the dark about the exact
nature of the emergencies. How do you and your
organization respond to emergencies? Take the following quiz and see how you do.

EMERGENCY ACTION QUIZ

Answer whether you agree or disagree with the following statements:

1. When faced with an emergency, we usually overre-
    act and rarely try to play it cool.

2. We've found that most of our emergencies are
    caused by unusual or out-of-the-ordinary customer
    requests.

3. The best way to deal with an emergency is to isolate
    the specific person, piece of equipment, or request
    that's causing the problem and fix it.

4. The types of emergencies we face are relatively
    limited.

5. We shield our customers from emergencies; most of
    the time, they don't even know anything went
    wrong.

6. We invite a lot of different people in to formulate
    approaches to specific emergencies.

7. Sometimes emergencies can't be helped; there are
    good reasons why we can't respond to emergencies

as quickly or efficiently as our customers or we would like.

CORRECT ANSWERS

1. Agree. Emergencies become routine for many organizations—consequently, they start underreacting to them. Far better to overreact than treat them as accepted and expected.

2. Disagree. Based on our extensive research, we've found that most organizations believe that their customers cause emergencies. In fact, most emergencies are rooted in faulty processes.

3. Disagree. Fixing an emergency isn't like fixing a leaky pipe. Though you might temporarily eliminate the symptom, you haven't treated the underlying cause of the symptom.

4. Agree. Most managers contend that they face an infinite variety of emergencies. In fact, the types of emergencies are few; they offer the illusion of variety simply because they happen so frequently.

5. Disagree. This is a major sin. Customers have the knowledge and the ability to help companies create effective strategies for handling emergencies; they also have a vested interest in doing so.

6. Agree. One or a few emergency "troubleshooters" won't do much good. Solutions come from interactions between employees from different divisions and departments. A broad-based group should be empowered to work on emergencies.

7. Disagree. Excuses are easy to make for emergency service shortcomings. We were understaffed, we couldn't have anticipated the large order, and it was a new customer. In fact, emergencies can be prepared for like anything else.

THE EVOLUTION OF AN EMERGENCY

Emergencies are caused by people falling asleep at the switch; they're more likely during periods of tight deadlines and rush orders; they're sparked by new technologies and procedures.

It's dangerous to make the above assumptions. Though they're partly true, they fail to recognize the role processes play in emergency situations. To help you recognize this fact, let me relate a typical emergency scenario.

A manufacturer of outdoor furniture receives a call from a retail account for a huge, unexpected order of lawn furniture; the retailer has suddenly discontinued their house-manufactured line and needs replacements by next month. The sales rep from the furniture company immediately calls his paint supplier, recognizing that he's going to have to move fast. He places a large order for ivory-colored paint—the color the retailer wants. The paint supplier rep scribbles furiously as he listens to the details. When he hangs up the telephone, he wants to go out and celebrate; the order is certain to cinch the company's salesman of the month award. He excitedly calls the order entry department and tells them about the order. The order entry guy is nervous; he knows that delivering such a large order in such a short period of time will be tricky. Before he can express his concerns to the rep, however, the rep hangs up. The rep sees his boss passing by and wants to tell him the good news. The boss is so excited that he gives the rep the rest of the day off. The next day, after some serious celebrating, the rep comes into the office and finds that his notes about the order are difficult to decipher. He's not quite sure about a few points. But rather than calling his customer and asking for clarification—he doesn't want to appear like he wasn't listening—he decides to forge ahead, figuring he's pretty sure what the customer wants. Little does he know that he's confused the delivery date with the shipping date, which will produce an emergency situation.

Now, let's change the scenario. The rep called back and got all the necessary information and passed it on to his order entry person. The order entry person, however, goes on vacation a week later, posting the instructions for the ivory paint near his computer terminal. But Joe, who knows to look near the terminal for post-it notes, is sick. His replacement doesn't pay any attention to the note, and an emergency ensues.

Now, let's change the scenario again. The order goes through cleanly, but no one remembers to tell the furniture company that the paint they're receiving has no lead because of the new EPA ban. This means that they have to bake the painted furniture at a higher temperature or it won't dry properly, leaving it vulnerable to nicks—and to emergencies.

Up and down the line, people will make mistakes, deadlines will be tight, and unexpected things will occur. The proper process will absorb these blows and will provide a cushion against emergencies. The wrong process, of course, immediately transforms the smallest mistake into the biggest emergency.

DESIGNING THE PROCESS AROUND THE SUPERIOR NEED

How does your customer define an emergency? Your sales team? Your customer service manager? Your engineers? What problems do emergencies pose for them? What would they do to handle them better?

Answers to these and other questions provide an organization with insight into the processes that work in emergencies and the processes that fail. Once again, what you're really searching for is the superior need. What emergency does the customer fear more than any other? What does he feel is the best way to avoid or solve it? Find the superior need and incorporate it into the process. If the superior need turns out to be overnight delivery, that need becomes the guiding light of the process. It means that the order processing people might have to sacrifice some time-consuming procedures in order to meet the overnight delivery goal. When you learn that customers believe that the worst thing that could happen is for delivery to take two days, you know the type of emergency that you want to avoid at all costs.

To discern the superior need in emergencies, ask yourself and your people the following questions:

1. If you were only able to fix one emergency in the past year, which one would it be?

2. If you were given the mandate to fix it, what would you do?

3. Of all the emergencies you face, which one causes the greatest problems for customers?

4. If you were in charge of the budget, would you be willing to pay a premium price to eliminate the emergency in 30 days? 60 days? 90 days?

Metra would like to welcome you and your family to our service!

Here are some safety tips for an enjoyable ride. Please:

- Stand well behind the yellow safety line on platforms.

- Keep young children seated with you and instruct them to stay with you at all times, particularly when you are boarding and exiting the train.

- Keep strollers and packages out of the aisle in order to avoid tripping hazards.

- Ask the on-board personnel for assistance if necessary. While they have responsibilities throughout the train, they will make every effort to assist you.

- Be prepared to disembark upon arrival at your destination.

- In order to promote family travel, we have special rates for families and children. We hope you enjoy your ride with us.

If you have any comments or questions, please call **Metra Passenger Services** at **(312) 322-6777 or RTA Transit Information at 836-7000 (city and suburbs), TTY (312) 836-4949.**

Metra
The way to really fly.

5. Do you think the solution to the emergency requires a deviation from a specific business process?

6. What is the biggest roadblock to handling an emergency?

7. Of mechanical breakdowns, product shortages, unexpected or unusual orders, and difficult time frames, which one is most likely to cause an emergency? Can you trace the cause back to a flaw in the process?

8. Is there anything your customers might do to facilitate your approach to emergencies?

9. What type of person is most likely to cause an emergency: a company employee, the customer, or an outside supplier? Again, can you trace the cause back to a flaw in the process?

10. If the emergency is not resolved and the customer is affected, what is the most common customer complaint?

Ask these questions of as many people as possible. Determine the superior need when it comes to emergencies. For some, the problem might be a system that can't accommodate large orders. For others, it might be a methodology that fails to tolerate the occasional, inevitable human error. For all, the superior need you must address is rooted in a process.

When an event inadvertently takes a company out of its process, an emergency is frequently the result. And nothing knocks the process for a loop more often than variations.

HOW TO PREPARE FOR VARIATION-CAUSED EMERGENCIES

Variations run the gamut. A company that usually orders 1,000 cases suddenly decides to order 100,000. A customer that traditionally orders industry-standard rectangular boxes decides that it needs triangular boxes for a new product design. But the variation doesn't have to be major to cause an emergency. Even a slight change can throw a process off.

To exemplify this point, let me tell you about my experience with McDonald's. They have a wonderful breakfast item that comes with eggs, sausage, fries, and a muffin. Or, at least it used to come with a muffin. Recently, and probably to improve their margins, they switched to a biscuit. McDonald's never announced the switch to the public; they just made it. Therefore, I was surprised and chagrined when I ordered this breakfast and found that they had given me a biscuit instead of the desired muffin. I was at a drive-thru window and told the order-taker that I wanted a muffin. After much gnashing of teeth and consultations with others, she told me to pull up and wait. About five minutes later, someone came out and handed me a cold muffin.

I couldn't resist conducting some impromptu research. I found another McDonald's and made the same request for a muffin. This time, the order-taker cast a cautionary glance around her, then quickly found a muffin targeted for use as an Egg McMuffin and handed it to me. I said, "You don't understand, I wanted the muffin instead of the biscuit." She shook her head and replied, "If I put the order in that way, you'll have to wait four or five minutes, and you don't want to do that."

There are right and wrong ways to handle variations. In the former instance, my request created an emergency—an emergency in which an order was unable to go through smoothly. Not only did my variation cause the order-taker to become upset, but I as the customer was also made to wait, treated somewhat rudely, and isolated away from the "normal" customers. In the latter instance, the order-taker was forced to break the rules in order to meet the superior customer need.

Obviously, the system was not prepared for this variation. There was no plan in place to deal with it. I'm sure in some instances, the order-takers simply refuse to substitute a muffin for a biscuit, creating the highest degree of customer dissatisfaction possible. This is the type of emergency where no one answers the alarm and a customer may be lost forever.

Here are the wrong ways to deal with variations:

♦ Ignore them in the hope that the customer won't notice the difference.

♦ Allow salespeople and other employees to deal with variations by the seat-of-their-pants, by using their best judgment.

♦ Fill the customer's request but tack on an additional charge for the variation.

♦ Fill the customer's request but make the customer feel like he's imposing or difficult.

♦ Fill the customer's request but make no preparation for dealing with other, similar variations.

Here is a four-step plan for handling variations:

1. Have everyone note variations in orders as soon as they come in.

2. Look for a common theme in variations—the ones that keep cropping up.

3. Examine the process and determine whether it's responding effectively to the variation-created emergency—are customers dismayed or delighted with the response?

4. If dismayed, reformulate the process so that it can cope with variations.

REFORMULATING THE PROCESS

It isn't easy, especially in these times of change and confusion. Revamping a process—whether it's the way salespeople are compensated or the way orders are entered into the computer system—is as scary as any change the company could contemplate.

But it must be done, and the way to do it is via the superior need. What customer need is your process failing to satisfy during emergencies? I know of a retail chain that became very upset with a supplier who shorted deliveries to the chain right before the Fourth of July weekend. The supplier, upon hearing from the very upset store buyer, responded heroically, sending his trucks flying out of the warehouse to other accounts and rounding up a sufficient number of units of the shorted products and delivering them in time to the chain.

It was a valiant effort. But it was only a Band-Aid. When the problem occurs again—and it probably will—the supplier might not be as lucky. His trucks might not be available or his other accounts might not be willing to help him out. The process has to change to accommodate the customer's superior need of no shortages during crucial selling periods. By exploring the options to meet this need and by having them in place when the emergency bell sounds, the supplier ensures that the bell will be answered.

There's another reason besides fear of change that makes it difficult to adopt new processes: the tollbooth mentality. The people who work at tollbooths have absolutely no incentive to work faster or more efficiently. No matter how quickly they make change or dispense travel information, they're always staring back at an unending line of cars. Naturally, tollbooth workers have absolutely no inclination to improve the process.

Workers at many American organizations feel the same way about emergencies. No matter where they look, they see a long line of emergencies. It seems like there's an emergency every second: if some assembly line machine isn't breaking down or the computer isn't on the fritz, some big account is changing their order in mid-stream. After a while, emergencies become the rule instead of the exception. Why change the process if there are all those emergencies lined up and waiting?

But the analogy isn't exact. Unlike cars at tollbooths, emergencies can be significantly reduced in number by an improved process. But everyone from lower-level employees to top managers have to be convinced of this fact. Once they shed their tollbooth mentality, they're much more receptive to process improvements. The odds are that someone in your company already has a good idea about how to improve the emergency-solving process. He just has to realize that his idea is welcome and that there's a good reason to improve the process.

Our firm has done a great deal of work with research and development departments, and I've learned an important lesson from them about employee attitudes and emergencies. About 80 percent of the work in the R&D lab is on management-directed assignments, and about 20 percent is on "flyers." Flyers are the R&D people's pet projects; they have to be hidden from management, because flyers take away time from what the lab is supposed to be doing. But the flyers also contain breakthrough ideas; they're the ones where scientists have invested their passions. Yet, these flyers don't see the light of day because the R&D people feel that they don't have a platform to launch them—which is too bad. Because process improvements, especially in emergency situations, often come from nowhere, from flyers. It's those ideas that nobody ever thought of before that solve the problem and that provide a way to cope with emergencies.

THE BLUE WHALE

In emergencies, we tend to focus on one aspect of the problem—one part of the process. When an order-taker writes that a customer ordered 5,000 units rather than 500, we respond to the emergency by firing the order-taker or by giving him a warning; or maybe we create a company policy that any order-taker who makes this type of mistake will be fired. The problem with such a response is that we're looking at only one part of the emergency, not the whole process that underlies it. We should revamp the process so that there is a system of checkpoints that will catch ordering mistakes before it's too late.

That we don't do so is a function of our modular mindsets. In our schools, we're taught via modules. A teacher takes a group through a series of modules, one at a time, and tests them on each module. If they pass, they move on to the next. Let's say there's a series of modules about the blue whale. One module teaches the class about the whale's evolution; another about its size, which is approximately 100 feet; and another about its feeding habits. The class learns a lot of facts about the blue whale.

But what if the modules were dispensed with, and the students were handed a ruler and told to go around the school and measure out 100 feet on the walls; to make a mark every foot until there were a hundred marks. As the children walk around the school, making marks on the walls, other students would probably come up to them and ask them what they were doing. They'd explain that they were show- ing the length of a blue whale. "Man," everyone would say, "that whale sure is huge." Every kid taking part in the measuring would grasp the size of a blue whale in a way that modular-taught students never could. They'd understand the blue whale as a whole rather than as a series of parts.

Seeing emergencies from the holistic perspective of the process rather than from the myopic view of an isolated fact makes all the difference in the world. With the former vision, emergencies are much easier to understand, to prevent, and to solve.

Chapter 8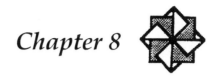

Research
and
Development

"*To be excellent, Company P needs to get involved in new production design earlier. They should be involved with future designs five years in advance. They should always be thinking of the future. They do work with us and are responsive, but I just don't see them looking into the distant future. They are fixed on the near (one or two years) future.*"

R&D departments used to be our strong suit. American companies were great at coming up with terrific ideas for new products and services. We seemed to have a genius for invention, a knack for building better mousetraps.

Then we lost the knack. Or so it seemed to many top managers who denigrated their R&D people, referring to their work as "art for art's sake" and calling them "scientists isolated from the realities of the business world."

MANAGER IN THE MIDDLE

If you're one of these managers, let me tell you about a test that we ask some of our clients to take after we've heard their complaints about their research departments. We ask a manager to sit in the middle of a room filled with chairs. Prior to this test, we asked the company's R&D people to write on slips of paper "urgent" assignments that they've received recently from executives in other departments. We then fill the room with people, handing each one a slip of paper, and they surround the manager in the middle. On the count of three, everyone shouts their requests at the manager, repeating the request for two minutes until a whistle is blown. At that time, the manager is told he has twenty seconds to pick the three requests that he's going to back during the next 12 months.

If nothing else, this exercise gives managers some empathy for what their R&D departments go through. This is not to say that research people are completely blameless for their plight. (As you'll see a little later in this chapter, they've contributed to the problem.) But the problem starts at the top and trickles down.

SQUANDERING R&D ON BAND-AIDS

If you're wondering where your organization's R&D dollars go, try this experiment. Divide a piece of paper in half. On one side, list all the precommercialization projects on which your research people worked in the past year. On the other side, list all the the post-commercialization projects. If you're shocked by the number of projects on the post-commercialization side, it's about time. R&D people are spending far too much time in the field applying Band-Aids when they should be in the lab developing wonder drugs.

There's a chemical products company in California that learned this lesson the hard way. Though their R&D center was in California, two-thirds of their sales force and technical support staff was east of the Mississippi. (Two-thirds of their market was located there.) When a new product was introduced, the technical support people had their hands full, ironing out a number of problems for customers. Unfortunately, communication between R&D and the technical group was poor; R&D had only a vague idea about what the tech guys were doing to rid the R&D-inspired product of bugs. Then an international competitor entered the market and raided the technical staff, stealing a number of key people. The chemical company, desperate to put people back in the field to help customers with continuing problems, simply took some R&D people from California and put them in technical support positions. Their rationale: "They designed the product, so who knows better how to fix it."

There was nothing inherently wrong with management's rationale, except for two disturbing consequences: (1) They seriously weakened pre-commercialization R&D efforts. By taking people out of the department for Band-Aid field work and by not replacing them, they placed the emphasis squarely on post-commercialization. (2) They learned that the technical people had been ad-libbing solutions to customer problems, often leading to worse problems down the road. The R&D guys were incredulous. If they had communicated better with the technical group, these horrendous ad libs might not have been made.

R&D people, however, have to shoulder their share of the blame. Their attitudes and outlooks account for some of the difficulties. The stereotype of researcher as ivory tower scientist contains some truth; the people in the labs can be a bit naive about the business world. Too often, they're easily manipulated by managers with their own agendas. Too often, they fail to pursue a course of action in the lab that is market-right but deviates from a given formula or set of instructions. All those years with beakers and test tubes can rob R&D people of a well-rounded view of their company and their customers.

On the other extreme, some R&D guys become jaded when exposed to the politics and game-playing of many organizations. They lose their idealism—their desire to find a scientific solution to a marketing problem—and they become little more than robots; they lack initiative. They've seen fellow R&D compatriots get cut off at the knees for bucking management with an off-the-beaten-path idea, so they cynically shut off their creativity and do their jobs by the numbers.

THE STEPS TOWARD A SATISFIED CUSTOMER

In the quest for great research and development groups, companies make many mistakes. Those mistakes include:

Hiring a guru. Unfortunately, gurus function best in speeches and when quoted by the media, not in hands-on situations.

Demanding home runs. Research and development is a game like baseball. A .250 average is acceptable. But many organizations expect an unreasonably high average of big hits. The fact is, any research & development group is going to have their share of strike-outs. You can't demand greatness where trial and error is the dominant methodology.

Prefering function to flyers. As the previous chapter demonstrated, "flyers"—the off-the-wall ideas R&D people come up with—often lead to breakthrough products and services. But management frequently brands these flyers as time and money wasters, preferring the many post-commercialization, functional tasks that routinely get dumped on R&D.

Avoid these mistakes. Even better, focus on following these steps:

1. Make a courageous commitment to the superior need.

2. Develop multi-disciplined teams to pursue that need.

3. Make and maintain contact with twenty vital customer relationships.

4. Verify on the cusp of commercialization.

5. Change the way management looks at and acts toward R&D.

A COURAGEOUS COMMITMENT

It's difficult for management to commit their R&D resources to a superior need. Because superior needs are not always the most obvious needs, they require a leap of faith, a kind of "build it and they will come" mentality. When, after long and assiduous study, you learn that your customers' superior need is Factor A, and for the past twenty years you and all your competitors have assumed it was Factor B, it's going to take a powerful commitment for you to tell your R&D people to redesign the product around Factor A.

In fact, it's much easier to aim for a secondary or tertiary need. It's far safer to jump on the research and development bandwagon, to test in the lab what all your competitors are testing. Of course, by doing so, you give up your ability to create a breakthrough product or service.

A few decades ago, Time, Inc., did a bit of research and learned that the "people" section of their magazine was an extraordinarily well-read feature; that it scored well above their expectations in readership surveys. It dawned on the powers-that-be that a gossip magazine about celebrities' lives might be a need that was going unfulfilled; it might even be a superior need. Such a thought, of course, ran counter to prevailing opinion. There were celebrity gossip columns, but no celebrity gossip magazines. But Time, Inc., made a commitment to research and develop one, and *People* became a magazine success story for the ages.

The automobile companies, on the other hand, resisted an emerging superior need for years. They refused to believe that their customers really wanted additional safety features like airbags, anti-lock brakes, traction control, reinforced side panels, shock-absorbant bumpers, backseat safety belts designed for children, and so forth. "They won't accept the tradeoff of higher prices for increased safety," many automobile executives privately opined. For public consumption, they made excuses about the difficulty of engineering safety solutions.

A company like Volvo recognized this superior need early on, gave a mandate to their R&D people to develop a car around the safety principle and carved an enviable niche for itself. The American car companies, seeing the superior need for safety grow and spread, scrambled to catch up, pushing their R&D people to help develop safer automobiles.

The lesson here shouldn't be lost on anyone: The earlier you jump on the superior need learning curve, the bigger and better your profit margins will be.

MULTI-DISCIPLINED TEAMS

R&D is the most homogeneous department in the company. If you study the resumes of your R&D people, you'll find that most of them took the same courses in college, followed the same career path, share the same interests, and read the same books. No matter how talented they might be as scientists and inventors, they own the same perspective.

That perspective needs to be leavened with other viewpoints. One way to do this is for management to turn R&D into a career stepping-stone for top management, rather than allowing it to be the end point for those with technical degrees. As a stepping-stone, R&D would attract English majors and salespeople, future CEOs, and entrepreneurs. Provide incentives for them to learn how R&D works and to participate in the process from a nontechnical platform.

It's especially healthy as a company grows. In an organization's early years, a technical genius or two in R&D often suffices. The company's technological innovation carries everyone on its back. Eventually, however, that technology isn't enough to sustain growth. A company like Wang rocketed to success on their technological creativity. Over time, however, they lost ground to competing organizations who could see beyond silicon chips to a bigger world, to superior customer needs.

Therefore, integrate your R&D department. Bring in people from sales, marketing, operations, manufacturing, and data processing. Have them participate in various initiatives. The mix would be healthy, creating debate and discussion beyond the technical parameters of a job.

TWENTY VITAL RELATIONSHIPS

To whom does R&D talk? In most instances, they talk primarily to other technical people. If they work for an industrial company, their contact is usually limited to their technical customer counterparts. If they work for a consumer products organization, they may never talk to a customer and they may receive customer information filtered through a dozen different sources.

Every R&D department should maintain close and continuous contact with customers. R&D people should be invited to sit in on focus groups, to interview customers in-person or on the phone, and to go out in the field and observe products in use in factories and homes.

Bringing your research and development employees and customers together isn't as difficult as it might sound. Begin the process by determining your twenty key customer relationships—your twenty most important accounts or your twenty best markets (demographically). Then find a way to create interactions between R&D and these customers. Be certain that the interactions are with the end-users of your products or services, not someone who is one or two steps removed from usage.

For instance, R&D groups at the automobile manufacturers are often woefully out of touch with customer needs. If you asked them if they were in touch with customers' concerns, however, they would answer affirmatively: "We always talk to the dealer service people and we look for patterns of problems in the claims that are filed." What they miss are the needs that don't show up on claims because someone other than the service department has Band-Aided a solution.

Let's say Joe buys a van, and shortly after the purchase he learns that he can't put a boat-pulling hitch on the van because the odd gas tank design is an impediment. Moving the gas tank, Joe discovers, will cost $1,400. Does he call the dealer's service department with a complaint? Of course not. He calls the salesman from whom he bought the van. After the salesman has his ears burned by Joe, he offers to call his brother-in-law, who has an auto repair shop, and have him move the gas tank, promising that it will cost no more than $200. Placated, Joe is satisfied. But other customers won't be satisfied because R&D isn't aware that the gas tank design is a problem.

Here's another example. An industrial battery manufacturer asks its R&D head if his group can design a battery with five times the power. The R&D head nods and says it's possible, and that research shows that customers want greater power from their batteries. Though I'm simplifying the process, the upshot is that R&D begins work on a more powerful battery. But if they left the lab and asked customers about a more powerful battery, customers might respond, "Sure, more power would be fine. Unfortunately, the big problem is the battery configuration, not the power. I've told your sales guy that a million times." But the sales guy hasn't told R&D. The best and only way R&D is going to get accurate and timely information is by going out and establishing communication linkages with twenty vital customer groups.

BEFORE TAKING THE COMMERCIALIZATION PLUNGE

Verify! Stop, look, and listen. Test. As tempting as it may be, don't rush a product out of the lab and into the market without first checking if your initial premise for the product is still valid. What looks great on the drawing board doesn't always work great when it takes tangible form.

I know of a can company that asked their R&D people to design a new type of paint can. The idea was to design a can that cost less to manufacture, sealed better, and was easier to open. R&D studied the problem and came up with a solution; namely, replacing the gnarled lip of the paint can top with a flatter lid that customers opened by inserting a special tool in a slot.

Excited about the new can, the company moved forward quickly, investing a great deal of money in a new plant to manufacture the can. But when the can hit the market, the market hit back. They complained that the absence of a gnarled lip caused the paint to slop over the lip and drip down the outside of the can, that they didn't have a special tool handy to open the can, and that the cans were hard to stack.

Without verification before commercialization, the can company didn't realize any of these problems would surface. In the lab, these problems weren't apparent. There wasn't time for verification of the can's efficacy in the field; there was no trial or testing period. The company was so confident in R&D's brilliant design that they rushed forward.

To avoid making the same mistake, test the actual product with customers and ask these verification questions before commercialization:

♦ Are there any unexpected or unanticipated reactions to the product?

♦ Are customers unhappy in any way with the product's packaging, design, speed, effectiveness, etc.?

♦ Is it possible for R&D to make a modification in product design to moderate or eliminate customer unhappiness?

♦ Is there any problem with product usage caused by "real" environments (versus the lab environment)?

REVISED MANAGERIAL APPROACH TO R&D

A change in attitude can do wonders for R&D, especially when the change comes from the top down. Here's how managers concerned with superior customer needs should think about R&D:

1. Be realistic in your expectations. Don't expect miracles, but don't err to the other extreme and accept only pragmatic technical work.

    Management tends to look at their R&D capability from a too narrow or too broad perspective. Broadly, they define R&D as a bunch of guys sitting at benches delivering the future. They expect great breakthroughs which is a foundation on which to build or rebuild the company. Narrowly, they view R&D as nitty-gritty problem solvers. They expect R&D to design a widget that works better, faster, more cost efficiently.

2. Give your R&D people a decent chance to make the right decisions rather than incentives to make the wrong ones.

    Some of the biggest R&D mistakes and missed opportunities arise because top executives hammer home the theme that cost is a top priority in product development efforts. I know of an R&D team that was designing a new plastic bag and chose a polymer construction material because their company made other polymer-based products and wanted to capitalize on economies of scale. It turned out that a competitor introduced a superior, nonpolymer plastic bag that "beat the pants off" this company, and the R&D team was called to task by management for failing to see that polymer was the wrong material for the job. Management conveniently ignored all the memos that they had issued about capitalizing on economies of scale.

3. If you have to kill R&D's pet project, at least give the researchers the opportunity to grieve their loss.

Talk to any researcher and he'll tell you how management "killed" a project, how an experiment suffered a "premature death," and how a vice president "knifed them in the back." The death-tinged metaphors convey R&D's frustration. Time after time, management launches them on an exciting project only to cut the journey short and to say that work has to stop because the marketplace realities have changed or that funds are lacking. None of this can be helped. But they can help R&D recover from the loss. A little common courtesy would be a good beginning. Managers should sit down with the R&D team and explain in detail why the project is being curtailed. They should also take some steps—and communicate those steps to R&D—to increase the odds that the same situation won't repeat itself. At the very least, these courtesies raise the low morale that plagues many R&D groups.

4. Keep the light bulbs on.

Negativity plays. The number of stories about how a powerful executive nipped a great R&D idea in the bud are legend. Every researcher will regale you with a personal experience in which a corporate honcho vetoed his idea for political reasons or because he didn't have the vision, courage or understanding to give it thumbs-up.

I don't care how brilliant or talented your R&D group. If they receive a steady stream of negative feedback from management, they'll never develop products around a superior customer need. They'll lack the energy and enthusiasm to do so. After a while, they'll get tired of rejection and criticism. They'll figure, "I don't need this. I'll just do what management wants rather than what I think the customer wants."

If you give your researchers a positive environment in which to work, you'll be amazed at how capable they are of homing in on superior customer needs. When management keeps the light bulb turned on and burning brightly, R&D can look beyond the lab to the outside customer world.

Chapter 9

Image

"*Suppliers today are trying to project a more market-oriented image, and they have succeeded to some extent. All suppliers use words like competitive, but I'm not sure they know what the words mean . . . it implies that a supplier is constantly searching for ways to improve its technology so that it can maintain or improve its ability to meet customers' needs. I'm not sure their actions dovetail with their words.*"

W hat's your organization's image? Are you a quality-conscious company? Innovative? Entrepreneurial? Customer-oriented? There are a host of possible adjectives that apply to your image. The following exercise will help you to determine what they really are:

On a piece of paper, list the ten adjectives that you feel best define your company's image. Then interview five people who are non-employees but at some point in the recent past have bought one of your company's products. Ask these people to provide a similar list of adjectives. Now compare your two lists.

Is your list significantly different from those of the people you interviewed? Problems of perception are common in corporate America. From CEOs down, organizational executives often have an insular view of their companies. The image they see is a result of internal propaganda, wishful thinking, and puff pieces in the media; they believe their own press clippings. It's easy to do. If you preach a vision of quality to all your employees, if you receive awards for quality, if the *Wall Street Journal* writes a glowing article about your quality programs, naturally you're going to think you're projecting a quality image.

Only the customer might not think so. Or the customer might not care. Maybe the customer thinks your quality image is fine, but your "shadow" image of arrogance and overpricing is not so fine.

The customer has a superior need relative to your particular products or services, and if you don't factor that need into who you are and how you're perceived, your image will be distorted. As we've stressed throughout this book, you should get a clear perspective on what your customers really want. If you determine that their superior need is fast, reliable, cost-effective service, a slick, premium image might hurt you. If your customers' major concern about your industry is that it's filled with customer-be-damned profit-makers, an image of trustworthiness might serve you well.

KNOW THYSELF

You have two choices when its comes to creating an image: either figure out who you are and communicate it to your customers, or figure out who you want to be and manufacture that image. Your choice, obviously, depends on the aforementioned superior need, marketplace realities, and competitive factors.

Never doubt for a second that you have an image or that your image is important. I've heard more than one CEO say, "Oh, our customers don't care about our image, they just care about our prices" or "We never have spent a dime or a moment on our image."

Every company projects an image, consciously or not, and every customer responds to that image, directly or indirectly. Just as people can't hide who they are inside, companies can't hide their souls. Like it or not, the core principles of an organization manifest themselves in many ways. The cutthroat competitor will be seen by customers as a hard-charging, aggressive company, no matter how the company tries to disguise these traits. Only if this company undergoes a major internal change—a transition of people and policies that brings in a kinder, gentler philosophy—will it be able to change its image.

Think about the images of major airlines. Most people believe that they're safe in United Airlines' and American Airlines' planes. Why is that? Do these companies send out a steady stream of marketing messages proclaiming, "We're safe, you won't get hurt on our planes"? Of course not. Their safety image flows from who these airlines are, their bedrock commitments. One of those commitments is to safety; it's their top priority. Without it, they'd quickly be out of business. Because their planes rarely crash, their image naturally connotes safety.

However when it comes to baggage handling, there is no similar, positive image. The airlines haven't made the same bedrock commitment to getting passengers' luggage safely from one destination to the next. Most passengers have experienced this problem firsthand. Therefore, there's a widespread negative image relative to baggage handling.

So if your image reflects who you are, why discuss the topic? Aren't we stuck with who we are? No! Though we can't ignore our corporate cultures and our traditions, we don't have to be their slaves. We can have a profound impact, both positive and negative, on how we're perceived in the marketplace.

BEWARE OF PANDERING TO THE SUPERFICIAL NEED

Numerous factors combine to create our company's images: advertising, public relations, promotion, packaging, customer service, corporate cultures, pricing, buying environment, distribution, and crisis management. The list goes on and on. If we fail to take each of these factors into consideration when communicating or creating our image, we will fall short of our goal.

Perhaps the single biggest mistake companies make in this area is to put an undue emphasis on advertising to shape an image. Like the rich man who thinks he can buy love, billion-dollar corporations sometimes believe they can buy image. They invest millions of dollars in a corporate identity campaign designed to give them a fresh image, a new look.

It doesn't work. Or, at least, it doesn't work for long. If the advertising campaign is the only tactic deployed against the image goal, it's bound to fail. If all the other factors discussed previously aren't incorporated into the image strategy, the advertising can't do the job.

Yet, we love to use advertising as our sole image tactic, especially in response to a market opportunity. In the past few months, there's been a significant amount of anti-Japanese and pro-American sentiment. Athletic shoe company New Balance, in response to that sentiment, began running ads that proclaimed their shoes were 100% American (unlike other foreign-made athletic shoes). Perhaps their advertising produced a temporary sales increase. However, by pandering to the superficial need, they hurt their long-term image. What's going to happen when the superficial need changes—as it always does? What if the market becomes enchanted by shoes endorsed by certain types of athletes? Or if there's a backlash against the shoddy quality of American-made running shoes? New Balance may find itself stuck with an inappropriate image. Or, they might find themselves creating a whole new image advertising campaign.

In either case, they'll have lost. When you pander to the superficial need, you invite customers to be cynical: "They're just jumping on the bandwagon." Or, you create an image that you have to take back a month later. The other problem is that changing your image advertising creates confusion among customers. You were pro-American last month; now you're neutral and emphasizing quality. In a few more months you'll be telling everyone that your shoe is fashionable, and is the one that's being worn by all the stars. Pretty soon, no one's sure what your company stands for. Your image becomes fragmented and ineffective.

HOW THE BOTTOM LINE DESTROYS POSITIVE IMAGES

We've been taught to sacrifice image for money. When the financial analysts tear apart a company for its poor quarterly earnings, the first things to go in the financial streamlining process are frills such as the idea people without line responsibilities, the beautiful new packaging concept, the state-of-the-art market research plan, and the consultants. We cut out the things that can enhance our image and try and get by with the "basics."

We've inherited this mindset from the educational system, which when faced with a budget crunch immediately cuts the frills; namely art, music, and so forth. Mathematics and the sciences, of course, are the basics and can't be touched. So we're left with people who can add and measure, but they've never been trained in aesthetics.

Yes, this is an oversimplification of the problem, but I use the analogy to illustrate how readily we sacrifice image to financial considerations. Perhaps the best example of this sacrifice is found in the changing image of the Ford Taurus. When this car was introduced, it enjoyed a superior image. It was perceived by many to be the ideal family car. It was a wonderful combination of luxury and performance. It was sufficiently adventurous and different to qualify as a middle-class status symbol of sorts. Needless to say, it became a highly profitable model.

But then Ford got greedy. Someone said, "We better load the plant." They increased production, flooding the market to get unit-buying pushed up because executive compensation was tied to meeting unit-buying goals. The rental market was the perfect place to soak up all these additional units, so Ford flooded the rental agencies with Tauruses. When that happened, the Taurus' image suffered. Rental cars are second class citizens; they're not status symbols or state-of-the-art models. The designer of the Taurus did not design it for the rental car market.

The lesson is don't take a visionary, high-margin product and push it into the commodity category for the sake of profit. If you do, your image—and eventually your profits—will suffer.

OTHER COMMON MISTAKES

Some organizations err in their image strategies for the following three reasons:

1. They believe their own publicity.

2. They try to latch on to a trend.

3. They insist on quick fixes.

The former error is commonly made by some of our biggest corporations. *Fortune* magazine recently had an issue about the companies with the best reputations in America. They determined who had the best reputations via a quick-and-dirty closed-ended mail survey. Even worse, they didn't ask any customers about these companies' reputations. Amazingly, they only surveyed the corporate employees themselves. The result, of course, was that the best known corporations received the highest reputation marks. Instead of reputation, what was really surveyed was name awareness.

But the result of *Fortune* magazine's survey and other surveys, media publicity, and advertising is to reaffirm to the top companies that their image is fine— that it couldn't be better. CEOs and other executives want to believe this is true; who wouldn't? Too often, however, the customer hasn't exercised his vote. Maybe all the surveys are right. But you should at least conduct the open-ended, customer-oriented research necessary to find out.

The second image error is latching on to a trend. There may or may not be a good reason to change your image. However, you change it because it seems as if you're going to be left behind if you maintain the status quo. In recent years, company after company has jumped on the quality bandwagon, competing for awards and other forms of recognition that will stamp them as quality companies. Quests for quality are fine. But it's possible that a quality image won't satisfy your customers' superior need. Maybe they're searching for a company with integrity; perhaps they would feel more comfortable buying from an organization known for its progressive stances on the environment and minority issues. It's possible that your quest for quality will backfire internally and that you'll use customer demands to bludgeon employees to perform at a higher level, turning customers into the quality police and creating an environment antithetical to customer satisfaction. Whatever the trend, don't hitch your image to it until you've done a lot of homework about your customers.

Third, don't panic and reach for a quick fix. As a consultant, I'm well aware of this tendency. Organizations recognize they have image problems, and they call us asking for help. But the help they want is often short term; their organization is perceived as poor service providers, and they want us to come up with a way to catalyze a 180-degree image turnaround in a month.

I have an analogy that puts this quick-fix mandate into proper perspective. The company is a sailboat, falling behind in a cometitive race with other sailboats. The sailboat owners call us, instructing us to "fill the sail with wind." We respond, "Well, we can do that, but we've inspected your boat and noticed that some frontboards are missing. You might have some seepage, which is why you're running low in the water, and you also have some barnacles. We think it would be a good idea to put in at dry dock and get the boat overhauled." And they respond: "We don't have the time or money. We're in a race, so fill our sails with wind."

Some consultants do exactly that. And while they might help a company get back in a competitive race, the image problems will eventually resurface to sink the craft.

A POSITIVE APPROACH: HOW TO CHANGE A NEGATIVE IMAGE

Organizations try desperately to change negative images. An old-fashioned company that wants to be considered contemporary brings out a flashy new product design. A company that's considered an environmental Neanderthal hires a public relations firm to communicate all the good things they're doing for the environment.

These knee-jerk reactions will probably fail unless they're tied into the superior need. If they are linked to that need, they can have a positive impact on image.

Perhaps you recall the shower attachments from the 1950s and 1960s designed to turn bathtub faucets into showers. They were a cheap-priced alternative to building a shower. Typically, these attachments were found in the hardware store, displayed in ugly, pressboard box packaging without a window and imprinted with the generic, Portable Shower Attachment. Not much to get excited about. But a number of years later, the company conducted some research and found that people who had traveled to Europe and used these shower attachments perceived them as upscale, exotic, and very European. Based on this research, the company redesigned their product, adding chrome and brass antique features so that it looked more upscale. They also renamed and repackaged the product, using a glossy black box with a clear polyethylene window. They took the product out of hardware stores and placed it in upscale department and specialty home furnishings stores. And, of course, they raised the prices. With this image change, the company tapped into a superior need and much higher margins.

A better known example is the transformation of Spiegel from bargain-basement mail-order company to upscale shop-at-home catalog service. The company, on the brink of bankruptcy, researched the marketplace in the mid-1970s and found that there was a growing number of working women who had more money, but less time to shop. In a remarkable turnaround, Spiegel jettisoned their old image of cheap merchandise for non-urban customers and targeted women executives, using many tactics to convince them that Spiegel was hip, happening, and service-oriented. Their turnaround is one of the great business success stories of recent times.

BUILDING BLOCKS

To get you into the proper image mindset, imagine that you're the owner of a medical products company. One of your main lines is aspirin. Now try a simple exercise:

On a piece of paper, list all the possible things that can affect the customer's image of your aspirin.

Compare your list against the following:

♦ Who my customers are—are they primarily older people who resent the child-proof caps that are impossible to remove if you have arthritic fingers?

♦ What influences my customers' buying decisions—is it past experience, a doctor's advice, a particular ingredient? Can you assign a percentage to each factor?

♦ How is distribution; is it convenient or inconvenient for most customers?

♦ What is the retail experience like? Is everything properly displayed? Are the sales clerks knowledgeable about the product?

♦ How does the product package look in the store? Do customers find that it's difficult to read the instructions, that the package is often dented or stained (from warehouse mishandling)?

♦ Do customers consider the price right for your particular product, or does it seem out of line in any way?

This is only a small sampling of the building blocks that you'll need to assemble your company's image. If you don't have one of those blocks—or if you have the wrong one—it can destroy the image you've labored to create.

If, however, you've got all your blocks together properly, the end result could be something like this.

A customer goes into a drug store and tells the clerk he has a terrible headache and asks where he can find the aspirin. The clerk points him in the right direction, but adds, "You know, if you're looking for something that really works fast, I've heard that Lytle aspirin is the best."

That's the power of image: it's so clear and pervasive that even the sales clerks get and communicate your message.

IMAGE-BUILDING INVENTORY

The following series of questions will enable you to assess your company's image strategy and determine what you've done right and what you've done wrong:

1. How have I determined my company's image? Has my company done the type of open-ended customer research that gives us a clear picture of how we're perceived by the people who matter most?

2. Is my organization's image in line with the customers' superior need? If it's not, have we done anything to change our image to bring it in line?

3. Have we defined what we want our image to be five years down the road? Have we defined it in terms other than economic? (Instead of simply wanting to

be a $2 billion company, you decide you want to be the company that produces the longest lasting widgets in the best product configuration and with the best service record.)

4. Have we committed any of the image sins discussed in this chapter: Pandering to the superficial need; letting bottom lines destroy image; believing your publicity; jumping on trends; and relying on quick fixes?

5. Have we built our image around a superior customer need; have we changed our image based on that need?

6. Are we fully aware of image's many building blocks; have we made an effort to make sure each image block is in place?

Chapter 10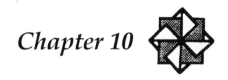

Customer Service

"When it comes to service, I expect the product I want, when I want it, the quantity I need and at the location I need it. We are . . . close to the bone in terms of the amount of inventory we can afford to have on hand . . . requires a continuous flow of material and I am alienated by a company that cannot provide the product in the needed quantity . . . because when we are out of product even for a short time we are brought to a halt."

Customer service is more than a phone line to answer customer questions and complaints. It is more than solving problems after the purchase has been made. It's more than a necessary cost.

Viewed holistically, customer service can be a tool to identify and to meet the superior need. Instead of a cost center, it can be a profit center.

To appreciate this broader definition of customer service, let's look at its three basic components, beginning with pre-transaction.

WHAT CUSTOMERS NEED BEFORE THE SALE IS MADE

Before you actually get a customer or before you sell an existing customer an additional product, you have the opportunity to provide him with service. That

service may come in the form of information by way
of advertising, direct mail, sales promotions or public
relations. Just as important, in the pre-transactional
stage you have the opportunity to form a relationship,
to set a tone for that relationship, and to establish the
ground rules. Customer service can be as simple as
informing a customer about the existence of your
product or as complex as creating a bond of trust and
respect between your company and the customer.

There's a superior need lurking in this pre-transaction stage, and if you can ferret it out, you'll be well
on your way to creating success. Consider the following list of superior needs that might exist in this pre-
buying stage:

- ♦ Need for basic information about product

- ♦ Need for technical information (how does the
  product work)

- ♦ Need for image, status

- ♦ Need for trust

- ♦ Need for conformity (others seems to be buying it, maybe it's time to jump on bandwagon)

- ♦ Need for human contact (to ask specific questions, to be reassured, etc.)

- ♦ Need for situational information (will it work
  for me in my situation)

It is not only what you provide the customer in
this phase, but also how. Specifically, do you entice,
delight, and intrigue? It's one thing to provide the
customer with the information he wants; it's another
thing to do so in a warm and engaging manner. In so
many of our pre-transactional dealings with customers, the dynamic is neutral. How many times have you
seen an ad that seemed overly slick, received a mailing
that was cooly promotional, and been approached by
a salesperson who seemed to be reciting a pitch from

memory? Whatever the superior need, it won't be met if we don't get our marketing approach out of neutral. As customers, we relish approaches that treat us as unique individuals, not as statistics on pieces of paper.

One of the biggest mistakes companies make in this pre-transactional phase is to fail to differentiate the audience. Different types of customers need different types of information. Here are some common types:

> **Quick Starts**—they just need to know a few pertinent facts before they make a buying decision.
>
> **Technical-Oriented**—they require hard data, like product specs before they'll move off the dime.
>
> **Middle-of-the-Roaders**—as the name implies, they require a moderate amount of information before they act.
>
> **Influenced-by-Others**—they respond to peer pressure and trends.

What type is your prospective customer? Are your pre-transaction customer service efforts targeted to the right type? To any type? Find the answers to these questions and you'll be that much closer to capitalizing on the power of the superior need.

DURING THE TRANSACTION

Let's say the customer makes it through the pre-transaction phase fully delighted. As a company, you've met his superior need and he's responded positively. Now, he's ready to buy. But when he goes into a store, the service dynamic changes dramatically. Perhaps the ad promised an upscale image, yet the distribution channel consists primarily of discount stores. Or perhaps a product brochure painted a rosy picture of a company's service capabilities, yet the sales rep contradicts that picture by hedging the brochure's bets. Or the public relations-planted story about your company's product made it seem like the product was wonderfully innovative, but when customers arrive at the stores because of the article, the salespeople are ignorant of the article and can't answer related questions.

You may still buy the product. But you probably won't maintain your delight. Your superior need during the transaction hasn't been met. Whether your need is for speed, or for additional information or reassurance, you've come up short. The odds are, you won't be a repeat buyer.

Credit card companies and other financial services businesses frequently commit the sin of "two-faced" customer service during the transaction phase. They send mailings that appear enticing and worthwhile; they're filled with information designed to help the customer evaluate the card's benefits. The language is clear and concise; the graphics are attractive. It's only when the prospect turns the mailing over that he finds mountains of fine print that state conditions and penalties in language better suited to a legal document.

If credit card companies were more upfront about the fine print and stated it in understandable language, everything would be fine. But burying all the conditions on the back in microscopic print violates the spirit of customer service relationships. Despite credit card companies' attempts to position themselves as helpful, customer-caring organizations, the fine print communicates another message to customers. It's like those old movies where the villain hands a widow a paper to sign, and when she points to the fine print and asks, "What's that?" the villain brushes her question aside and replies, "Oh, that's nothing. Just sign."

When credit card companies do the same thing, they destroy the service dynamic. Sure, there still might be a short-term relationship. But they've decreased the odds for a long-term one.

AFTER THE SALE IS MADE

What's wrong with your post-transaction customer service? Look over the following list:

♦ Busy signals or put on hold when calling customer service

♦ Service department slow to solve the problem

♦ Service department makes things worse trying to solve problem

♦ Customer service rep is rude, abrupt, stupid

♦ Customer service rep doesn't really listen to complaint and responds inappropriately because he didn't listen or ask for clarification

♦ Customer service department does everything by the numbers, providing customer with easily forgettable experience

These are all common customer service problems. Many of these problems are caused by management's perception of customer service as a necessary evil: it exists to fix mistakes, not to contribute to the bottom line. In many organizations, there's an insidious resentment against this department, and the resentment shows up in how the department is run. Typically, positions in this department are poorly paid, and the work force is often poorly educated and transitory. Training is unimaginative and rudimentary. Customer service reps are taught how to answer different types of calls, where to get specific types of information, and when to kick the customer up to a higher level.

Then, when they're ready, they're placed in a harshly lit room, assigned an uncomfortable chair, given insufficient information to handle the technical questions, and forced to endure complaint after complaint. Worst of all, they're rarely empowered to solve a problem. Even when they can come up with a solution, they're forced to say, "I have to talk to my supervisor" or "I can't do anything about that right now."

If you recall my analogy from a previous chapter about the people who collect tolls, you can see the same frustration here. The incoming calls are like that stream of cars—there's no end in sight and no incentive to do the job better.

As a result, customer service people have great difficulty discerning the superior need. It's easy to make false assumptions about callers' needs. It's easy to believe that the only thing that will make a complainer happy is her money back, and to figure that the only response that will satisfy a confused customer is a chat with the head of engineering. But the real need, the superior need, may be finding someone at the other end of the line who empathizes with their plight. They might require nothing more than a sympathetic ear as they complain. Maybe someone else's need is just to hear a customer representative say, "I'm sorry, we made a mistake."

Unfortunately, in this post-transaction phase, most customer service employees aren't trained to listen for that superior need or empowered to do anything about it.

A SIMPLE FIRST STEP

Independently audit your customer service dynamic, from pre- to post-transaction. You can do this with an independent research firm asking the type of open-ended questions discussed earlier. But you should supplement their efforts with your own grass-roots effort.

Specifically, do it yourself. An amazing number of employees have never bought any of their company's products (at least through regular channels of distribution). Role-play the typical customer. Find an ad or other marketing vehicle that makes you aware of the product. Write down your reactions during this pre-transactional stage. Are you enticed? Is there sufficient information? What sort of feeling does the marketing engender? Are your expectations raised?

Next, buy the product in the usual way: a store, by mail, by way of the phone. Observe and note every aspect of the process and your reaction to it. Are you delighted? Do you have buyer's remorse seconds after making the purchase? Is the buying environment meeting your superior need?

Finally, contact the customer service department with a question or complaint about the product. Again, write down your feelings and observations. Is the process smooth and efficient? Is the customer service rep listening and responding appropriately? Are you getting your questions answered to your satisfaction? Is something being done about your complaint that will make you delighted?

When you're done, you might want to have a few other people go through the process and keep the same written journals. Compare their entries with yours. Look for common themes and for the possibility that the superior need is going unmet.

THE 25 QUESTIONS

What are the 25 most asked questions of your customer service department?

If you don't know the answer, find out. You'll learn that of the 25, five are technical questions, ten are related to installation difficulties, and ten are complaints. Within each of these three categories, prepare data so that your reps have it on hand to give customers. Computerizing this information will greatly accelerate the answering process.

Though this is a good start, it won't take your customer service department to the next level. It may satisfy customers, but it won't delight them. The superior need is not only what you say, but it is also how you say it.

Your customers operate in different modes. Some assimilate information best through their ears; others, with their eyes; still others can assimilate data well with either ears or eyes. Then, there's a fourth group that assimilates best when they combine "touch" with one of the other senses (e.g., the customer needs to try to put the product together as the customer service rep gives him instructions).

Training your customer service representatives to discern the particular mode of a customer is not as hard as it sounds. If reps simply ask the customer such things as, "Do you want to get the product in front of you before I explain what to do?" or "Would you like me to send you a written letter duplicating what we just went over?" that will enhance communication and customer satisfaction.

CUSTOMER SERVICE AS A SELLING OPPORTUNITY

Management views customer service departments from the narrow framework of speed and efficiency. It's rare that they see the broader potential for their departments—the potential for profit. Yet it's there. It's there because customer service provides organizations with the opportunity for customer contact, often at the instigation of the customer. Instead of merely responding to the customer's complaint or request for information, why not use it as a springboard for another sale?

There's a wonderful opportunity to migrate customers up the cost curve. Once they've bought something from you, and assuming they're delighted with the relationship, they're excellent candidates to buy something bigger and better. It's a natural progression, and you see it in categories such as jewelry, furs, and art.

But you're not going to be able to take advantage of it unless you broaden your view of customer service. One of the ways of doing so is to ask these questions:

♦ What written, telephone and in-person contact did your customer service department have with customers in the past year?

♦ Based on all the complaints and information requests, what were the recurring themes (e.g., people love everything about the product except for flaw X, or customers wonder why they can't get the product to do what the advertising promised)?

♦ Based on the recurring theme, what customer need was going unfulfilled?

♦ At the point of customer contact, could you have sold the customer a product or service that would have met that need?

♦ If so, how might the customer service department best incorporate a sales pitch into their
system?

GIVE CUSTOMER SERVICE PEOPLE THE FREEDOM TO BE HUMAN

The worst customer service departments are those that
are forced to simulate computers. Deprived of their
ability to be spontaneous, to be flexible, and to be
decision-makers, service reps simply process data.
Though they may respond courteously and appropriately to customers, they never establish any rapport.
Though they might recognize the customer's superior
need, they lack the authority, freedom, and incentive
to respond to it.

How can you humanize your customer service
group? Here are three suggestions:

1. **Free them from the do's and don'ts.** Get rid of the
   rules and regulations that hamper their ability to
   respond to customers. Rules, such as "you will
   spend no more than one minute with a customer per
   call" or "you will deal with Type A complaints in
   the following way," must be abolished. It's fine to
   have guidelines, but they should not restrict the
   rep's relationship with customers.

2. **Give them enough information to talk intelli-
   gently.** Reps sometimes talk to customers like robots because they haven't been given proper or
   sufficient information. Customer service people feel
   stupid when they aren't prepared for customers'
   questions, and they set themselves on automatic pi-
   lot in order to avoid dealing with their lack of
   knowledge.

3. **Let them improvise.** Allowing your people to use their common sense and creativity is essential. Most people can guess from a customer's tone of voice, words, and specific problem what they need. Rather than providing the standard answer or course of action, an innovative, instinctive reaction might better meet the superior need.

A few weeks ago, a friend of mine went into a dealer to buy a motorcycle. The salesperson recognized that although he knew something about bikes, he wasn't capable of doing major repair work. After he bought a 1200 cc bike—twice the number of cc's as his previous bike—the salesperson brought unexpected and unasked for people into the customer service dynamic; namely, other motorcycle buffs who knew far more than he did about mechanical and maintenance issues. They helped him to "break in" the bike, gave him tips on what to do if something went wrong, and told him to give them a call if he needed any help.

He was delighted. His superior need for sources of advice and repair assistance was met. The salesperson provided him with customer service that was humanistic in the best sense of that word. He factored in who he was and tailored his approach to his particular situation.

IMAGINATION AND EXTRA CREDIT

Doing something *extra* and doing it *imaginatively*. If you want to turn your customer service department into a stellar performer, these are two important ingredients.

Doing something extra has always been and will always be the hallmark of service. It's what General Electric does in its post-contact reviews. After you call their customer service center, they get back to you two days later and ask you a few questions in order to verify that the service they provided met your needs. It's when the service representative not only promises you a replacement for a defective product, but also delivers it to your doorstep within the hour. It's when your request for information is met by someone who not only supplies the data, but also does so in a friendly, genuine, and enthusiastic way.

Imaginative customer service might seem a contradiction in terms. What could be more cut-and-dried than customer service?

It doesn't have to be. In fact, it can be your competitive point of difference and your unique selling proposition. Consider a company that's selling a commodity or parity product. The service dynamic presents an opportunity to gain a competitive edge. Let's say you're selling bags of salt. Why not place inside the bag a card with a toll-free number for people to call and learn about salt efficiency (in water softeners) for their area of the country?

The imaginative delivery of valuable information frequently delights customers. For instance, there are hundreds of thousands of people with sensitive skin—skin that's irritated by certain compounds dry cleaners use on shirts. What if a shirt manufacturer created a booklet for skin-sensitive customers; namely, a booklet that told customers what shirt fabrics to avoid, how to wash them, and so forth?

Again, delight. There's no guarantee that imagination and extra effort will hit the superior need. But combined with the other tactics discussed in this chapter, you'll find that you're closer to the target than ever before.

Chapter 11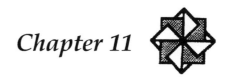

Two Cautionary Notes

L ike any powerful tool, meeting the superior customer need requires practice to maximize its
power, If you're like most people, you're going to be
a bit overconfident after your organization puts it to
the test. When you see the impact of the superior need
(e.g., improved market share, better customer relationships, increased revenue, etc.), you might think,
"Not only does this work, but it's also easy."

It is, and it isn't. Compared to may theories about
customer satisfaction, the superior needs is relatively
simple to comprehend and implement. In fact, the
process is seductive. I've seen a number of organizations become convinced that the superior need was a
panacea, rather than an ongoing process. Once they

identified and met their customer's superior need,
they sat back and counted their mounting profits. A
few months or years later, however, they never saw
the truck that hit them or the competitors that carried
their customers away.

To avoid this unfortunate position, keep these
two problems in mind: First, resist the temptation to
harvest the field sown by meeting the superior need.
Second, keep a myopic eye trained on the customer
and don't fail to watch the manufacturing and marketing resource allocation ends of the business.

HARVESTING

When you meet a superior customer need, you build
activity equity. All your activities that helped you
meet that need (i.e., marketing, manufacturing, customer service, etc.) become equity. The investment
you made in those activities is now paying off; you've
become highly effective and efficient as marketers,
manufacturers, and so forth.

At that point, you have a choice you can continue
to grow that equity, harvesting your profits slowly but
surely, or you can grab every dollar you see as soon as
it sprouts from sales.

An astonishing number of organizations choose
the latter option. American Express is a perfect, recent
example. Not too long ago, American Express could
do no wrong, In fact, four years ago we profiled the
credit card market for a client, and we found that at
every level we checked, American Express was the
definition of quality. People were willing to pay
higher feed because they understood and accepted the
dynamic that was in place. Clearly, this market leader
had found a way to meet the superior need.

Then everything changed, And American Express is now struggling with fierce competition, re-

tailer protests, customer dissatisfaction, and decline share.

Did American Express become complacent? Not at all. In fact, just the opposite occurred. Certain managers saw the opportunity to capitalize on short-term opportunities. Having met the superior need, they were in the perfect position to push aggressively for results that would make them look good and lead to promotions and perks for selected managers. At American Express, a group of managers created a strategy that increased customer charges, expanded the number of accounts and used the American Express name to move into other areas (e.g., travel services.) Combined with a number of other tactics, American Express' financial picture couldn't have looked better.

But the activity equity they were using up in their quest for profits and promotions came back to haunt American Express. By harvesting what the superior need had sown, they left themselves open to criticism and competition.

HOW ARE YOUR PEOPLE COMPENSATED?

In most American corporations, compensation formulas reward individual success. Similarly, success is often narrowly defined as increasing return on investment in a given period, regardless of the long-term, negative impact of "success." Incentives are in place for managers to push money to the bottom line, advance their careers, and ignore the future.

If you change the compensation system, you eliminate the harvesting incentive. If executives are compensated for meeting the long-term needs of the organization, harvesting ceases to be an attractive option for career opportunists.

DISCERNING THE SUPERIOR NEED MORE THAN ONCE

The point of this chapter isn't to stop ambitious executives in their tracks. It is to help your organization meet the superior need not only now, but also in the future.

A perfect analogy is found in sports teams. Some win a championship only once, while others create dynasties. The former get caught up in the euphoria of winning and fail to keep in shape in the off-season. They worry more about endorsements than goals, care more for individual statistics than team performance. Dynasties like the Chicago Bulls and the New York Yankees simply don't take their eye off the goal. Year in and out, they do what it takes to keep winning.

Meeting the superior need over time is the same as building a sports dynasty. You're not satisfied with that one moment of glory. As of this writing, the superior need among automobile buyers is safety. Many can manufacturers have responded to this need by installing a driver's air bag. Some companies will no doubt harvest this superior need. They'll install them for all passengers, they'll increase the prices to build margins, and they'll tout their air bags as safer than other air bags.

Other companies, however, will discern and meet an evolving superior need related to safety. Volvo is already doing so by advertising their crush cages and reinforced side panels as providing protection not afforded by air bags.

Searching for the superior need is an ongoing process, and the only way to search effectively is to be attentive to the voice of the customer, As I've emphasized throughout the book, that voice changes, and if you don't have monitors in the marketplace to listen, you'll base your customer satisfaction strategy on old voices.

DON'T DO IT BY THE NUMBERS

When companies meet a superior customer need, they frequently follow up with a big price. The customer demand for your product is higher than it's ever been. Distribution is expanding rapidly, and you're getting great aisle and shelf placement. All your research confirms that you've met or exceeded customers' expectations, and you're the category leader by many lengths.

According to pricing theory, a 20 percent price increases is justified. Or is it? Here's what happens when a big increase is pushed through. At first, everyone is happy. More money is pouring into the company's coffers than ever before. Over time, though the company creates a pricing umbrella under which competitors camp. The huge price increase allows competitors enough pricing room to gain a foothold on the market that capitalizes on the resentment that your big increase created and provides an alternative for customers who can't afford your new price.

And it doesn't end there. Competitors can translate their increased revenue into marketing resources (i.e., more advertising, public relations, promotions, a better sales force, etc.) to attack the market leader.

When you meet the superior customer need, therefore, raise prices less than the "formula" says you should. Instead of 20 percent, maybe it should be 12 percent. Obviously, you need to increase it enough to give a reasonable return on your investment. Just don't become greedy. You want to raise prices just enough so that competitors don't have sufficient room to slide in and steal a segment of the market at an attractively lower price.

THREE TEMPTATION-FIGHTING TACTICS

It's difficult for many organizations to resist harvesting. The pressure on public corporations for quarterly gains is tremendous, and it's easy to say, "I've got to make the bottom line look better."

Before yielding to temptation, rely on the following tactics:

♦ **Translate organizational knowledge into income.** There is more than one way for companies to make money. They don't have to devalue the superior need to boost revenues. Instead they can translate their "intellectual property" into ancillary profit centers. Any organization that meets a significant customer need will naturally build activity equity. They will obtain hard earned knowledge about a customer problem or opportunity, and they can market that knowledge.

For instance, an environmentally responsible manufacturer hits on an innovative solution to decrease plant pollution. Most companies would show the dollars spent to create this solution as a compliance cost on the balance sheet.

I'm suggesting this cost be turned into an asset. Why not set up XYZ Consulting Engineering as a subsidiary and market the pollution solution to other manufactures?

Why not? Because organizations continue to define their business narrowly; they're convinced that they're only manufacturers and can never be environmental consultants. It's time to develop a broader vision of who you are as an organization.

♦ **Don't let the senior staff make all the decisions.** Decision making is often isolated among top management and financial people. Middle managers and line workers are shut out. This latter group is closet to the customer and the marketplace. They should be allowed to say, "This move creates this problem, and that one this opportunity." Strategic planning is top down, which was fine for the pre-quality era. But in an era where customer needs are paramount, planning should be from the bottom up. This will help prevent decision that help the bottom line but hurt customer relationships.

♦ **Don't be so quick to shoot the bad news messengers and reward the good news proclaimers.** When Ross Perot told General Motors that there was something wrong because Ford at half the size makes twice the money of GM, top management perceived him to be a cantankerous meddler and bought him out in order not to have to listen to him anymore. Perot was saying, "Don't harvest just yet' we have a problem." Unlike Perot, most employees are reluctant to point out problems with customers for fear of censure or worse. Fostering an environment where any news about customer concerns is encouraged will help the organization listen to the customer voice.

At the same time, be wary of career opportunists who look great on paper. I'm sure that you know someone in your organization who has received accolades from the CEO for his group's results, and it's only months or years later when everyone realizes the numbers came at a price. He might have improved his share more than any other product group, but he also created tremendous animosity among customers along the way. Before passing out the accolades, let some time go by and research how the paper numbers translate into customer satisfaction.

LOOK BEYOND THE CUSTOMER

I've probably used the word "customer" more than any other in these pages. While meeting the superior customer need is the most important aspect, it's not the only aspect. If you fail to keep track of your manufacturing and marketing resources allocation as compared to competitors, it won't matter if your meet the superior need form now until the end of time. You're still going to come up short.

Cost gap analysis a term used to describe the difference between your capabilities and those of your competitors. First, let's look at manufacturing gap analysis.

Here are two examples, one positive and one negative, that illustrate the importance of manufacturing gap analysis.

A recent Ford annual report noted that they had analyzed manufacturing costs at their plants and at those of their competitors and determined that the five top plants (in terms of lowest costs) were Ford's. If General Motors had figured this out a few years back, they might have been sufficiently alarmed that they wouldn't have paid out dividends and pursued other harvesting actions. Instead, they would have been rightfully alarmed and figured out a way to get their plants up to speed.

Motorola, on the other hand, examined the manufacturing cost gap analysis in the pager market and determined that there was an alternative process that would result in dramatically lower costs—far lower than even the Japanese companies. After adopting the new process, Motorola became the market leader and is doing especially well in foreign markets, including Japan.

Foreign companies tend to be lower cost production than American companies. When you get past all the superficial reasons for this problem—lower pay scales and more innovative approaches to productivity—the real reason emerges: we do relatively little gap analysis. How many American organizations have searched for the lowest cost producer in a category and vowed to drive costs even lower? Very few, I'd bet.

The same problem exists with marketing resource allocation. Let's say that you run a large corporation with a 100-person direct sales force. One day, you hear about a much smaller competitor who is using telemarketing and a videotape as its major marketing tool. A few people make calls and each averages many more sales per month than your best salesperson.

Given such a scenario, it may be time to reassess and reallocate your marketing resources. One of the great sins committed by U.S. corporations is staying with established resources too long; namely, resources that no longer are effective for a changed or changing customer base. Why do we commit this sin? There are a number of reasons, including:

♦ No one is willing to stand up and say, "This isn't working." In the previous scenario, the salespeople won't say anything because they fear that the may be endangering their jobs or those of co-workers if they suggest that telemarketing is working better than direct sales.

♦ Traditions are hard to break. Companies grow attached to their marketing strategies; they love them beyond all reason. Part of the problem is the old saying, "You got to dance with the one who brung you." Top managers convince themselves that they shouldn't forsake the marketing formula that brought them success, ignoring the fact that the marketing environment has changed dramatically. There's also a general mistrust of "newfangled" marketing methods.

♦ Failure to listen to the customer. Do your customers feel your salespeople are crucial to the process? Could they do without them? Would they prefer to communicate with you by mail, phone, and fax? What percentage of your customers remembers or has seen your advertising; if they remember it, did it have any impact on their perception of your company or is products? These questions often go unanswered. Or they're answered with "yes's" and "no's" in response to closed-ended questions, giving organizations precious little insight into what customers need from marketing.

THE DECLINE AND FALL OF OBSOLETE ASSUMPTIONS

Never take anything for granted, especially the old organizational assumptions of the past. The cautionary notes sounded in this chapter are designed to help you to treat all assumptions with healthy skepticism. They should enable you to keep a sharp eye on those who might harvest your company's activity equity. It's no longer acceptable to do so. They should also prevent you from resting on your customer service laurels. Having happy, satisfied customers is great,. but you also must compare your manufacturing costs and marketing resources allocations with competitors if you expect them to remain happy and satisfied.

I was recently in Toronto, and watched the news in a hotel room. A reporter came on and started talking about the economic dark ages in Toronto, while he gestured at an enormous tire warehouse complex behind him. At one time this tire warehouse served all of Canada, over one-half million busy square feet. But as the technology of tire changed and improved, there was no need for this huge warehouse space. On the television, the space looked forlorn and deserted: it was a symbol of the industrial decline of the Western world.

However, I happened to know the portion of this space had been converted into offices for hundreds of companies, each with fewer than 50 employees. Each of these companies was in the service business, selling a broad range of ideas and knowledge rather than products. They are among the fastest-growing, highest margin businesses in Canada.

The unintended irony of the reporter's commentary should give all of us pause. Don't buy into the idea the American (and Canadian) companies are on an inevitable downhill slide and that they's nothing to be done to reverse the process. Through it's true that large organizational structures are becoming much smaller, that doesn't mean that the end is near. Rather, it signifies that we need to adapt to a new order, as the new service businesses in Canada have done.

To adapt, discerning and meeting the superior customer need is obviously necessary. But as you do so, don't make the same assumptions about harvesting, manufacturing, and marketing that others have made for years. It's time for a fresh perspective, and I hope this chapter give you a new way of looking at old issues.

Chapter 12

Selling Your Organization on a Superior Need Strategy

I t's not always easy. I've found that the concept of a superior need, like any untried approach, often encounters resistance. It may be the CEO or a particular department or a level of management that resists. In many respects, it's easier finding out the superior need than finding a way to sell management.

This chapter provides you with a list of the objections that you're likely to encounter when you propose going after the superior customer need. It also offers you some "tried and true" methods for countering these objections and gaining acceptance for this unorthodox approach to customer satisfaction.

OBJECTION #1:

THE SUPERIOR NEED IS A GREAT CONCEPT, BUT IT IS REALLY NOT APPLICABLE TO US BECAUSE WE'VE ALWAYS BEEN CUSTOMER-DRIVEN

Variations on this theme include: "Our founder built the business on the idea that the customer comes first, and we've never lost that philosophy." Or: "Our salespeople are in the field all the time talking to the customer, so we know what's going on."

Many organizations have a customer-first philosophy. But very few dig below the surface to unearth the superior customer need. If you run into resistance because management is convinced that they know everything about the customer, ask them if any of their salespeople has told a sales manager something like the following:

"I just want you to know I was at our top account today for our annual review. Everyone was there, and I have to say they're not pleased with our responsiveness; they don't like our typical 48-hour turnaround delay. Of course, I could reduce that delay if I didn't have to be out selling all the time. Another problem with my busy schedule is that I haven't kept up with the industry, so my technical expertise isn't what it should be. They called me on that and also on the fact that I don't always deliver what I promise."

It doesn't happen. Your salespeople aren't completely honest with you because it is not in their best interest to tell the whole story. In addition, it could be that their customers aren't being honest with them. Our research shows us that customers often avoid major confrontations with suppliers, pretending that everything is fine until they switch suppliers.

If you propose a superior need approach and you're rebuffed with comments about how everything you hear from the field tells you customers are happy, try any or all of the following three tactics:

Interview five salespeople or store clerks who left your organization in the past year. They'll be brutally honest with you about customer relationships. If they articulate a problem, there's your ammunition.

Interview five ex-accounts. Again, you'll receive information from them that you won't get from current accounts. They'll tell you why they left, and if you spot a recurring theme in their comments, you'll have an inkling about where you've gone wrong.

Circulate copies of the above interviews among customer service, manufacturing, marketing, and other departments. You can build a lot of support this way for an alternative customer satisfaction strategy.

OBJECTION #2:

IT COSTS A LOT MORE THAN OTHER TYPES OF RESEARCH

Closed-ended research costs less. The open-ended questions designed to capture the voice of the customer involve a more complex process. The superior need isn't always obvious; it requires a good deal of probing and analysis before it emerges.

Still, these facts often don't sway objections from the cost-conscious person. What does sway them is a demonstration of value, as the following example demonstrates.

We have a client who thought they were providing good value to the marketplace, but it was only a thought. They had no way to verify that value. But they needed to verify it when they were contemplating a significant price increase. If the value wasn't there, their customers would rebel at the perception of price gouging. We took a snapshot of the marketplace for our client, of the needs and expectations of their customers, and at how their competitors were doing.

We found that our client's value stream was 20 percent greater than any competitor. With that knowledge, they were able to create and implement a price increase strategy with confidence. Management was able to brush aside objections that the financial community would come down hard on them for the increase and that customers would desert in droves. The evidence of the healthy value stream was irrefutable. Everyone in the company from top managers to engineers to financial executives was energized by the evidence. They instituted a price increase that added $28 million to their bottom line in the first quarter.

Combat cost objections with a simple truth: information is worth its weight in gold. It was worth $28 million for our client. If you can determine how customers value your products and services versus those of competitors, you'll gain knowledge that will make virtually any strategy you pursue more effective.

OBJECTION #3:

WE HAVE A QUALITY PROGRAM IN PLACE THAT WILL SATISFY OUR CUSTOMERS

Great. However, don't confuse quality with customer satisfaction. If you doubt that statement, take a look at recent Malcolm Baldridge Award winners. While they've scored very well in most categories, customer satisfaction isn't one of them.

The quality movement doesn't ensure that you'll do the right thing; it only ensures that you'll improve upon what you're currently doing. That's fine. It may well move your customer satisfaction scores from average to good, or even from good to excellent. But it won't get you to "delight."

Even the best quality improvement program is limited from a customer standpoint. After all, quality began as a way to reduce product defects and evolved into cultural attitudes and philosophy. In most cases, quality cascades down from top management to the mailroom.

The voice of the customer, however, cascades up. In quality programs, it's easy to miss that voice or to hear it faintly or to fail to communicate what's heard throughout the organization. When the voice is heard in a quality program, current or old customer needs are captured. The superior emerging need often escapes management.

Why? Because the quality movement usually doesn't place an emphasis on the type of open-ended, probing interview methodology we've discussed. The emphasis is on improvement, not on qualitative information. The time, effort, and analysis necessary to discern the superior need are lacking.

Therefore, if someone in your organization objects to this quest for the superior need from a quality position, explain that quality and customer satisfaction aren't synonymous; and that if you can meet both, you'll create a synergy that will greatly benefit the organization.

OBJECTION #4:

IT SOUNDS GREAT, BUT I'M WORRIED THAT IT WILL TAKE FOREVER TO GET A SUPERIOR NEED PROGRAM UP AND RUNNING

Yes, a series of linked but unscripted questions take longer to ask and answer than a seven-minute, yes or no survey. And yes, analyzing open-ended responses takes longer than quantifying close-ended ones. Generally, you need to allocate about ten weeks for the research phase of a superior need program.

But that's not forever. What can take a long time and what every organization should guard against is the phlegmatic post-research phase. You should have a system in place to handle the superior need information that starts flowing across people's desks. Lengthy delays often occur because of the following two problems:

Unpreparedness. It is not enough to do the research; you have to be ready to act on it and set up and empower cross-functional teams to implement strategies. It's only after the research is done that organizations begin the process of responding to it. That's when they distribute the data, build consensus, reassign people to respond to what was learned, and develop action plans. This process can take a year or longer, and by the time the team is ready to move, the research is no longer valid or management has lost interest.

Disbelief. More often than not, the results of open-ended, probing customer satisfaction studies are startling. They reveal things about customers that organizations never knew or even contradict accepted notions. As a result, management may react with disbelief and discount the data.

To avoid these problems and counter time-based objections, take the following steps:

1. Get your empowered cross-functional team in place and working simultaneously with the research effort. Don't try to put the team together or build consensus at the last minute. Don't wait until the information about the customer arrives before you realize that the manufacturing member of the team

has another project in which he has to participate. As soon as the superior need is spotted, the team should be ready to design and to implement a strategy to capitalize on it.

2. Prepare a plan to communicate necessary changes to the work force. As a result of what you learn about an emerging customer need, you may have to make changes within your organization such as revamping job descriptions, reorganizing departments, reassigning, eliminating, or adding job responsibilities. As soon as possible, create a way to communicate these changes to the work force so they understand why the changes are necessary and what their roles are in the process.

3. Double-check the research for skeptics. This third step is especially true if you anticipate disbelief from certain sectors of the organization. We routinely hire an independent third party to interview the customers that we have interviewed. They evaluate how we did. The results of this independent audit are then passed on to our client. Assuming we did our job professionally and thoroughly, the results will be reassuring to organizations and facilitate implementation.

OBJECTION #5:

THE HEAD OF DEPARTMENT X WILL NEVER BUY THE SUPERIOR NEED APPROACH

If you suspect a specific person or group will resist the superior need strategy, there are a few ways to melt that resistance. The resistance may come from people who are happy with the closed-ended approach that the organization has used for years. If so, invite them to attend an open-ended session. At first, they may react negatively, saying such things as, "Our (closed-ended) research firm allows us to push a button and listen in on any one of 150 telephone interviews, and we can follow along by reading a copy of the script."

What we've found, however, is that their prejudices decline as they hear the voice of the customer, often for the first time. People who sit in on our telephone sessions bring pencil and paper, intending to write down what they hear. But they soon stop writing and start listening as the discussion between customer and interviewer increases and takes off. The discussion can get "wild and wooly." After all the interviewing is completed and the data analyzed and translated to report form, we show it to the people who have sat in on the session. They're usually amazed at how what they heard has been converted into useable superior need information. They, too, have been converted to open-ended research advocates.

Another tactic is to tempt resistant people or groups with specific benefits associated with superior needs. For instance, a prospective client was interested in changing their delivery initiative. They came to us and asked how what we offered differed from our competitors: "You give us a score on delivery, and so do they," the prospective client said.

We responded that we also provide a prioritized group of eight to fifteen steps that will meet customers' superior delivery need, and we'll price each step against the potential gain to determine the cost-effectiveness of each step. You can't do that with research that fails to discern the superior need.

Bringing up potential cost-savings from a superior need strategy is still another way to dissolve resistance. One of my associates was meeting with a large industrial company, and they were talking about the firm's problem with lead time. Because the company's industry was in a downturn, some executives at the meeting were reluctant to proceed with our proposed research plan. That reluctance quickly faded when my associate asked a simple question: "If you could cut the industry standard lead time in half, what would you get?" "An immediate $40 million gain to our bottom line," the company's financial executive responded. When you find the superior need, you often realize significant profits.

OBJECTION #6:

OUR CUSTOMERS DON'T HAVE A SUPERIOR NEED

Every organization's customers have a superior need: it's just not always obvious at first glance. I guarantee you that I can find a superior need in at least one of our categories (e.g., product quality, price, emergencies, and so forth) for any company, no matter what product they produce or service they provide. Even customers for commodity products like sugar, soap, and salt have superior needs.

How can I be so sure? Don't some customer groups have a number of equal needs? Look at it this way. How does a buyer choose between alternatives? What makes him pick Brand X instead of all the other brands? Because Brand X satisfies his superior need more than any of the others. It may be that Brand R satisfies a number of subordinate needs, but quantity is no substitute for the real thing.

People in your organization may claim that there's no such thing as a superior need. If so, ask them to try an experiment. Tell them to ask a few friends about a recent purchase . The purchase can be expensive or inexpensive, product or service. Specifically, ask why they chose the product or service over others in the category. The odds are that each person will offer one, distinct reason: "It was less expensive than the others" or "I liked the way it looked." But even if they provide a litany of reasons, a little probing will reveal that one supersedes all the others.

Obviously, this is an oversimplification of the research process, and it's prone to error, but it usually gets the point across. A superior need exists, and if you ask the right people in the right way, you'll find it.

OBJECTION #7:

THIS ISN'T THE BEST TIME FOR US TO DO THIS TYPE OF RESEARCH

Too many things are happening to go off on a superior need "wild goose chase," some people in your organization might say. We have all these other projects going on; the last thing we want to deal with is another project. On top of that, you've just downsized and the industry is in a downturn. You should be cutting back programs, not expanding them.

The counterargument is: Your competitors are in the same position, and whoever gets to the superior need first wins. Everyone is vulnerable and weakened because of the excesses of the 1980s and the recession. Everyone has cut back. Everyone has only a certain number of dollars to invest. In the 1980s, you could invest those dollars in expansion strategies, capital equipment, and people in an effort to serve more customers better. Today, you need to invest in information. In the near future, market research dollars will equal or surpass the research and development expenditures of most organizations. Information will give you a competitive edge.

It will not only give you a competitive edge, but it will also give you a sense of how customers are responding to your downsized, reorganized company. All your relationships are at risk. If you've cut back or replaced your sales staff, you may have lost vital links to customers. If you've taken out a layer of management, you may have lost some crucial "idea" people who forged the image to which your customers respond.

OBJECTION #8:

WE DON'T WANT TO BE THE FIRST TO TRY THIS; MAYBE IF OTHER WELL-KNOWN COMPANIES HAD EXPERIENCED SUCCESS WITH THIS TYPE OF APPROACH . . .

Throughout the book, I've offered examples of organizations who have profited from a superior need strategy. In some instances, however, I've deliberately refrained from identifying those organizations—quite understandably, they don't want competitors to get wind of their strategies.

I recognize that real names will be helpful for readers who want to convince their managements that a superior need approach is a tried-and-true one. Therefore, let me provide you with three brief case histories our clients have approved for publication.

Morton International's Automotive Safety division has become the dominant player in the air bag market. They've done so by viewing the quality issue from a superior need perspective. That perspective dictates that they have a better understanding than their competitors of what *all* their customers require— not just original equipment manufacturers, but employees, aftermarket providers and especially suppliers. Over the years, Morton has invested in superior need research that has given them tremendous insight about what's critical to vendors. As a result, they've maximized the effectiveness of their air bag componentry. But they've done so not only through traditional technological channels, but by listening and responding to what their vendors said would *really* result in a better relationship and a better product.

Nalco Chemical Company used a superior need approach in an entirely different context. Listening to the customer voice, they heard that customers were concerned about the traditional steel drums used by the chemical industry to ship and store product. When they became aware of this concern, they probed and questioned; that posed "what if" scenarios; they used a variety of open-ended techniques to discern the superior need.

When they found it, Nalco's top management authorized a team to embark on a quantum leap improvement. The result was the patented Nalco Porta-Feed Advanced Chemical Handling System. They were able to distill the critical concerns of customers into one unique product. For instance, these containers featured sloped bottoms for full drain, preventing the chance of any residual chemical; they were also the first containers in the industry to be owned, recycled and maintained by one company; and a computerized tracking system was created to track all shipments.

Customers were delighted. Nalco's response to a customer concern went far beyond the norm. The typical response might have resulted in some improvements to the drums that were currently on the market, marginally improving storage and shipping specs. Instead, Nalco made the effort to learn not only what would satisfy their customers but what would be the ideal solution to their problems.

Third, let me tell you about the extraordinary investment Inland Steel has made in trying to hear what's most important to their customers. In most organizations, you can count the customer relationship touchpoints with your fingers—there's the sales-customer relationship, the customer service rep-customer relationship, and so on. Inland Steel has identified 47 touchpoints and is in the process of building a system that will give them unprecedented access to their customers' needs and expectations throughout each of those points. From what they've already learned, Inland Steel has the blueprint for manufacturing technology that will enable them to produce in one day what it takes their competitors seven days to manufacture!

Finally, here's one more reason to act now rather than later. Customer needs are changing at a faster pace than ever before. There's a superior need just starting to emerge in one of your customer segments. Your salespeople haven't spotted it, your traditional research hasn't tracked it, your customers may not have even articulated it. But it's there. Any organization that fails to monitor and respond to these rapidly changing customer needs is going to be left behind.

Chapter 13

Superior Questions,
Superior Needs

Though the specific questions you ask your customers as you try to discern their superior need will vary, certain common lines of questioning will work for everyone. In this chapter, I'd like to provide you with some tips about the kinds of questions to ask and how to ask them by dividing them into categories. This is by no means a definitive list, but it should offer you some helpful hints that you can use.

PRODUCT QUALITY

In this need category, most companies are obsessed with meeting specs. They labor under the assumption that if you've met the spec, then you've met the superior need. Certainly, specs are important. But they're only the starting point for meeting customer needs, not the ending point.

Which brings up our first question to ask customers:

What attributes are critical to your specification of product quality as it relates to product x? List them in order of importance.

In the customer's mind, there's a prioritized order. It may be that he considers product quality in terms of speed, durability, and efficiency, but which one comes first? Not only that, but how did he arrive at his specifications and their ranking?

From where did the specification come? Did you generate it yourself? Was the process deferred to a specifying engineer? Have you accepted the industry norm?

We take so much for granted with specs. That's why I generally ask the following question:

Who certifies compliance with the spec?

If they say, "I leave it to my supplier," then that gives you valuable information not only about how they determine product quality, but also about the trust the customer places in his supplier. If the customer responds, "I check every one myself," it says something about the lack of trust in the supplier. Many other questions along this line can be asked, especially about sampling and sampling ratios.

Now let's turn to some questions that stretch the definition of product quality. It's a stretch that just might give you a clue to a customer need that your competitors have missed.

What do you require in the product "look," including surface appearance and packaging?

Aesthetics have a lot to do with the perception of product quality. For some supermarket customers, quality is only present when an apple's skin is gleaming or a head of lettuce is free of blemishes. Some customers associate quality with a buff finish, while others believe a certain color is most prestigious.

What type of environment do you plan to use the product in?

Is it going to be used in an aerospace environment, or used commercially? Is it going to be used in the desert or in the mountains? Will it receive the majority of its usage in a high tech or low tech factory? Sometimes, the environment doesn't matter—e.g., when the product functions equally well in rain, wind or snow. But sometimes, it will be adversely affected by certain conditions. Or it may be that it functions a bit better in dry rather than humid conditions. If the bulk of your customers are in Mississippi, that subtle fact may turn out to be a superior need.

What type of person will be using the product?

Your product may be as technologically sophisticated as anything to come down the pike in years, but if your customers are technologically unsophisticated, they'll wonder out loud why you've made your product "so darn complicated." Learn what your customers know, and who they are in relationship to your product. If they're young hotshot engineers and your product relies on an old, established design, they might view your product as an anachronism. Know your corporate customers in the same way. Some organizations like Texas Instruments prefer receiving products in component form rather than assembled; they're more comfortable putting it together themselves. To them, components equal quality. To another company, it may indicate something else.

Product quality questions reduce to physical product properties, aesthetics, environment usage, and customer characteristics. Don't neglect any of these areas, and you won't miss the superior need.

DELIVERY

As noted in the delivery chapter, this is the easiest customer need to satisfy. But it won't be easy if you fail to ask the following question:

What constitutes complete and delightful delivery in your mind?

Not partial and adequate delivery. Complete and delightful delivery point the way toward superior. From an industrial standpoint, it may be the front gate, the loading dock, next to a machine, and at an inspection point. From a consumer perspective, it may be on the front porch, in the mailbox, and in your hands. There are many possibilities, and you should try to analyze the one that completely delights your customer.

Who in your organization keeps track of delivery performance? And how?

You may be delighting the wrong person. Your questions should help you to identify the specific person at a customer's organization who you have to satisfy. Once you have identified that person, you have to figure out how he measures your performance. Some questions along that line include:

Who tracks delivery performance among your various delivery sources?

Is it tracked via a formal system (a computerized system) or is it tracked informally (someone is keeping track in his head)?

What is the process for communicating dissatisfaction with delivery performance? How does it get initiated? What are the stages?

Finally, ask a question that will help you formulate a strategy, if you're currently failing to meet your customer's superior delivery need. Too often, organizations in this position struggle to mend their ways, only to find that they're not rewarded when they do so. To avoid that possibility, use this question:

If we can move our delivery performance from dissatisfaction to delight in your eyes, how can we ensure that you'll give us the proper credit for investing the time and energy to meet your needs?

EMERGENCIES

It's easy to get misleading information in response to your emergency questions. As soon as you mention the word "emergency" a customer will recite a number of examples. Unfortunately, many of them may have nothing to do with real emergency needs. They're ones he's heard about from others. Emergencies fuel the gossip pipeline in organizations, and as the information flows, it becomes distorted.

Therefore, a critical question is:

Based on your personal experience what constitutes an emergency in your mind?

You might want to follow that question with:

Where are the different places this emergency originates from?

Of these places, rank them in order of most common to least common.

Of the emergencies you've mentioned, which one is the biggest in terms of dollars? Which is the most frequent? Which is the one that falls between the cracks (frequent enough to be annoying, but not frequent enough for your company to have developed a way to deal with it)?

At this point, you may have culled some of what you need to know to pinpoint the superior need. But usually, there's a big piece missing. Emergencies are difficult for customers to discuss for a variety of reasons—there hasn't been an emergency recently, or they're removed from the resolution process, or they have so many emergencies it's difficult to sort one from another, or emergencies have become an accepted part of doing business. To complete the picture, you need the customer to help you flow chart the emergency process—from inception to resolution. Ask questions that help you trace the chronology. Don't neglect the resolution options—the various alternatives available to customers to solve the emergency problem.

Once you've finished the flow chart, put it in graphic form and show it to the customer. In most instances, visualization of the process will trigger additional information you missed initially. The customer will point to something on the chart and say, "Hey, I forgot to tell you about this step here."

At each point in the flow chart, you want to get the following information:

Who's involved at this point?

What is required of this person's involvement and why?

How fast does this person respond and what resources does he or she rely on in the response?

If this person can't respond, what's your backup option?

Pose hypothetical questions to solve the customer's problems. If the customer complains that it takes five days for a supplier to respond to product shortages, ask what if the supplier could respond in two? You might evoke a delighted response.

After a customer states that there's no back-up person for an employee who is at a critical juncture of the flow chart and that if he's not there, the emergency response time doubles, you might ask:

What if your supplier had someone who you could call 24 hours a day to help you in case your main contact was out?

He might respond, "That would be great, since I stay up nights worrying about what would happen if our computer went down and he wasn't available. But he'd have to get back to me within a few minutes and implement action within the hour. I'd pay anything to have that peace of mind."

Suddenly, you have the parameters for giving your customer peace of mind and meeting his superior need.

PRICING

Searching for the superior pricing need requires questions that dig below the obvious numbers. Below the surface you'll find a customer value stream that has a lot more to do with pricing needs than manufacturing and marketing costs and competitors' prices.

Begin to search for that stream by eliciting what elements the customer feels he's getting in his purchase. If someone is purchasing a fur coat, the dialog between interviewer (I) and customer (C) might go like this:

I: What was the main reason you bought the fur coat?

C: For warmth.

I: How warm?

C: What do you mean?

I: It keeps you warm to ten below zero, twenty below?

C: Twenty below sounds right.

I: What about durability? How long do you expect it to last?

C: Oh, ten years or so.

I: Is there any other element you expect to get out of your purchase?

C: Well, fashion.

I: What do you mean?

C: When I hand the coat to my host at a party—I go to lots of formal parties—I know she's going to look at the label, and I want her to be impressed.

In this dialog, you might capture a nugget of information that allows you a pricing opportunity. For instance, if the customer in the fur coat example noted that she was somewhat skeptical of a fur coat company that claimed that their coats keep wearers warm up to 20 below zero, you might ask her that if a recognized testing service guaranteed that claim on the label, would that affect her willingness to buy one brand over another and to pay a little more for a coat?

From the elements customers believe they're getting, move on to the values. Probe the values. You want to find out why customers value certain elements more than others. You might learn, for instance, that fur buyers value mink for its warmth over all other furs because their mothers told them it was warmest. If you're selling deerskin coats, you can use that knowledge in your advertising, by perhaps beginning an ad with the line, "Mother doesn't always know best." The superior need may be for customers to receive reassurance that it's "okay" for them to buy a cheaper, yet equally warm coat.

You'll also want to probe the emotional context of a customer need. If you price against the logic of your research—77% of respondents say they will pay more for a product with material x in it—then you're flirting with disaster. Emotion wins the pricing battle over logic every time. For instance, my son destroys the knees of his jeans with alarming frequency, so we naturally gravitate toward buying jeans made of heavy material at a relatively low cost. He still wears out the knees, but not quite as quickly as with lighter jeans. If an interviewer asked me if I would pay more for a better quality pair of jeans for my son, I'd probably say no, based on my assumption that he's going to ruin them. But if someone probed, he would discover the problem with the jeans and ask, "Mr. Lytle, what if we gave you a 12-month, money-back warranty on the jeans, would you be willing to pay $5 more?" At the question, my emotion would kick in and I'd say, "$5? I'd pay $20 more if I thought the knees wouldn't be ripped for a year."

Finally, don't be afraid to wander with your price questions. We've found that the key to a customer's superior pricing need may be located quite a distance from the expected spot. One of the ways to track down the key information is by asking questions that move out of the product category and into the more general class. If you're the aforementioned fur marketer, you may want to ask a question such as:

What's the last premium product you bought that disappointed you? How did it disappoint?

You may learn that the reason customers aren't willing to pay $2,000 for your coat is because they bought a top-of-the-line air-conditioner last year that has never functioned properly. The superior need isn't for a lower-priced fur coat, but for evidence that a negative premium purchase experience won't be repeated.

RESEARCH AND DEVELOPMENT

One of the most critical areas of questioning and one that is often neglected focuses on the internal customer. What does your R&D department think of past initiatives. By their responses, you'll quickly discern if you're meeting the superior need or, if not, where you're going wrong. Begin this way:

How did your last major R&D initiative originate?

Prepare yourself for multiple, often conflicting stories. Still, try and sort fact from fiction by asking what critical piece of information, trend or event prompted the initiative. What was the catalyst for staff or budget approval? What options were explored when the project began?

Then, move to the "trigger" question:

Based on your experience, what other options should have been explored?

Through that and related questions, you want to reveal the screens through which the initiative passed (e.g., product durability, materials, application, profitability, size of total market potential, company strengths, distribution, current customers, and so forth). Figure out what screens should have been used but weren't. Based on the customer's responses, ask the following:

In your opinion, how can you quickly and cost-effectively take what you've learned from the initiative to meet someone's need?

You'll be surprised at how much thought most R&D people have already given to this question. In many cases, they will tell you about how what they've learned can be applied to tap into a smaller market—one that is less ambitious but no less viable than the one originally targeted. The superior need can often be found in a more narrowly focused customer base.

Here's a high anxiety question that I would caution you against using until you've established some rapport with your customer:

If management said to you that they would give you and your team a chance to buy your R&D effort at reasonable terms, would you put any of your personal money on the line?

Yes, it's a loaded question. But it just might reveal what your internal customer really thinks about the company's ability to satisfy customer needs through research and development.

COMPANY IMAGE

The attitudinal questions here are relatively obvious and easy:

Within the context of the product category, who has the best quality, the best service, and the best responsiveness?

However, this type of question will only get you so far; they may even mislead you about the type of image that prompts customers to buy. That's why superior need methodology demands that you take the customer through behavioral modes by way of examples. Your research may indicate that customers trust Maytag more than any other appliance company because of the image created by their lonely repairman ad spokesperson. But they buy Sears because it's easy to get a Sears repairman out if the machine breaks down.

Many of the big research firms ask attitudinal image questions such as "What brand has the greatest visibility?" and "Who has the most memorable advertising?" Through the answers, they give all sorts of brand recall and attitudinal scores. But they're not always relevant, since many products with lousy image scores are market leaders.

Test attitude against behavior with hypothetical questions. For instance, tell the customer to place himself in the following situation: he's flown to Hawaii for a national sales conference but his luggage is lost; his boss tells him he has a $300 budget to buy a tennis outfit for a game with a key account rep. Given this situation, ask:

What brand of shoes, shorts and shirt would you buy?

Then shift gears with real life questions:

Who bought you your last pair of tennis shoes? What brand? Why did you decide you needed them? Have you been satisfied with their performance?

Juxtaposing hypothetical situations with past experiences helps you to identify conflict points. In the first scenario, the salesman might buy a brand of shoes to impress his tennis partner. In the past, he may have never bought that brand, and you should determine why. What image triggers his buying impulse?

The way to find out may be to ask a paradigm question that gives you a sense of how he behaves when confronted with a certain image.

Pose the following situation to a customer: he decides that he wants to play basketball to stay in shape, so he begins looking at basketball hoops. Then ask:

Would you buy one where you have to assemble it yourself or would you have someone else install it? ("I'd assemble it myself, since I'm a closet do-it-yourselfer.")

You have two choices of types of equipment. They're both basically the same, but one has a picture of Michael Jordan embossed on it and it's a little more expensive. Which would you choose? ("The less expensive one; I really don't care about which celebrity endorses things.")

Contrary to what you might expect, the point of these questions is not to determine what basketball equipment the customer would buy. It's to determine what athletic shoe image satisfies his superior need. He obviously is not concerned about the borrowed interest of having an athlete connected to his product (so he probably won't buy Nike). He certainly responds positively to a product that offers him the chance to participate (so he may buy the Pump shoe from Reebok).

Yes, this is an oversimplification of how this type of paradigm question works. But I think you understand how it functions. It reveals how customers respond to certain images.

One last point about image. The customer's superior need may be different from the person who influences (or even makes) the buying decision. Men may fall under the spell of those Old Spice commercials that promise a wild, romantic adventure with a beautiful woman. But when a husband and a wife are shopping and the man reaches for the Old Spice, the woman may knock his hand away and say she refuses to let him buy that "sexist" stuff.

That's why you should always find out who the buying influencers are in a household or company, and how image affects their attitude about and behavior toward a given product.

CUSTOMER SERVICE

The first questions should help you to understand the customer's definition of customer service. You may want to help him along with some leading questions related to your product, such as:

What was the last time x broke down?

What type of experience did you have the last time you called the toll-free customer service line?

How helpful were the instructions when you were trying to fix it yourself?

Sometimes, especially in the industrial sector, people are reluctant to talk about customer service. They may feel uncomfortable complaining, or they may not like to admit that they don't know what to do when something goes wrong and they need help. A few prompts are in order such as thrusting the customer into the seller's role. Some prompts include:

Pretend for a second you're the customer service manager for Company X. What would you do if . . . (a common customer service problem).

Ask questions that explore the nuances, because the superior customer service need often lurks in the corners. Certainly, you want to learn if your subject wants service faster, more efficiently, or more courteously. But go after the nuances with questions like:

If you could determine how you would receive customer service, would it be by phone, mail, fax, computer or in-person?

Would you like to receive product instructions on paper, audio, video, or computer diskette?

When and where are you most likely to use the product?

In response to this last question, the customer might reply, "Well, I'll tell you, I'm using my computer to write a movie script, which I do late at night, and when I need help and call the software company's helpline, no one answers." The superior need is for someone to be staffing the line after midnight.

Questions that get customers to relate recent service experiences are especially instructive. Unpleasant experiences often roll off the interviewee's tongue, and you can spot the unmet need quickly. Therefore, always explore what happened when your subject last had a customer service need.

WHAT TO LISTEN FOR

In this chapter and throughout the book, I've asked you to take a different approach to customer satisfaction. Many of the questions in the preceding pages aren't being asked, are being asked in the wrong way, or the answers are being unintelligibly translated into a yes or no statistic.

It is not enough to meet basic customer needs; you have to search for alternative ways to discover the superior need. You can do so in many ways, though I've found that the telephone is the best tool for obtaining information with relative speed and ease. It is well-suited to the open-ended approach that I advocate.

Over the years, our clients have used this approach strategically to capture that elusive customer need. We've helped our clients to analyze and to interpret responses to the questions and to formulate plans that have achieved highly ambitious objectives faster and more effectively than ever before. Once they have identified a superior need, everything else seems to fall into place.

Let me leave you with one final tip about how you can identify that need. After you've asked your questions, listen to the answers from two perspectives. Listen to the literal meaning—what the customer is saying. However, also listen to the tone, the intensity, and the emotion of the response.

There's a certain pitch that signals delight. You'll hear it emerge in all sorts of ways; namely, in the way one customer can't stop talking about a specific subject, in the way another customer suddenly becomes animated in response to your "what if" question, and in the way a customer's language becomes positively poetic (instead of doggedly prosaic) when he comes to a certain topic.

Keep your ear tuned to delight. You'll know it when you hear it; and when you hear it, you've found a superior customer need.

Chapter 14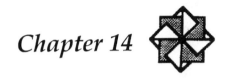

Beyond the
Superior Need

Discerning superior customer need is like discovering a map containing clues to buried treasure—what you have in hand is potentially valuable, but you still have to translate it into action for the information to pay off.

Though I've provided translation tips throughout the book, I cannot overemphasize how important it is to do the right thing with the right information. Doing the wrong thing—and there are countless wrong things to do, from playing politics with superior need data to underfunding a program based on that data—will always cause you to miss the customer satisfaction mark.

In the final chapter, I'd like to give you some tactical advice about doing the right thing. I've divided the tactics into two sections. The first focuses on how to proceed after you come upon that amazing superior need information—the steps that will maximize the value of that information. The second section suggests some more general tactics, enabling your organization to maintain a superior need focus despite all the distractions.

POST-NEED STEPS

1. **Put your team in place so they're ready and waiting to respond.**

    I've said it before and I'll say it again; get your people ready so that when the superior need emerges, they'll be able to react quickly and effectively. I've seen many organizations fail to respond to superior customer needs, not because they didn't know what those needs were, but because they weren't prepared to respond. Sometimes political in-fighting slows down the process. Sometimes the problem is fear or uncertainty.

    Designate the people who have the skills and authority to turn what the customer says he wants into actual programs. Create a team. Empower the team to act as quickly as it can once it receives the necessary information.

2. **Put the information you receive into an ROI format.**

    This will be your best defense against the naysayers and doubters within your organization. When you discover what your customers really want, put that information into dollars invested versus dollars returned. Clearly document the money that must be invested to meet that need and what your probable return on that investment will be within a reasonable time frame (one or two years).

If you fail to do this, you're going to be forced into a weak position. There are people in every organization whose decisions always relate to short-term profit, and no matter how compelling the customer need, it will take a back seat to costs versus gains.

3. **Bring the superior need to the right people within your organization.**

This is a difficult one to coach from a book. When clients ask me to help them build support for a superior need strategy within their organizations, I'll always ask a number of questions to help me pinpoint the right people. In lieu of asking those questions, let me list the characteristics shared by people who tend to support superior need strategies:

- ♦ They're open-minded—they never automatically turn down a project or program just because it's unusual or different.

- ♦ They tend to be working on other initiatives that challenge the status quo in one way or another.

- ♦ They've pushed through projects that everyone said would never make it—they possess the energy and commitment to lobby long and hard for something they believe in.

Two other tips that will help you secure proper internal backing:

- ♦ Look for a reasonably high-placed executive that you're closest to (in your department, group, division, etc.). Though he might not be the perfect person to support your initiative, if he has the characteristics described here, his circle of business "friends" probably includes the perfect person. I've found that people with these characteristics network in most organizations. So take the easy route and approach someone you've established a relationship with, and ask that person to help you recruit others.

♦ Request backing for the superior customer need initiative by posing a question rather than making a statement. Experience has taught me that there's a certain skepticism to superior need data. When people learn that customers want something unexpected or unheard of, they often back up a bit and start questioning. To lessen that skepticism, pose hypothetical questions to your targeted "backer," such as: "If we had a $40 million opportunity that would fall to the bottom line within 20 months, would a $10 million investment make sense?"

4.   Always document the superior need journey.

Keep a written record of how your customer need research evolved. This data is volatile—it can easily migrate away from you and from your group. It can become a political football, and everyone starts claiming possession. A written record helps you keep a measure of control. It enables you to refer back to exactly what the customer said he wanted; if you happen to get roadblocked or if there's some dispute about the customer's stated need, this record will be a valuable resource. In addition, your team may change; new people may be brought in. A written record helps get everyone up to speed quickly and reduces the chance of miscommunication.

5. **Keep talking to the customer even after you've elicited what he really wants.**

Once you capture the superior need, you will turn you energies to getting a program or project off the ground. That's fine, but don't forget that customer needs change faster than the weather. Keep track of those changes via a constant customer dialog. Regularly ask customers "what if" questions—what if we added feature y, would you pay x dollars more; what if we made it three times faster, would you buy it over brand x?

Contrary to popular belief, ongoing research of this type doesn't require an enormous budget. We recommend that our clients eat lots of snacks between big meals—that is, do major research projects every year or two, and in between conduct highly targeted, quick-hit projects that simply keep you aware of any changes.

Maybe this approach to research costs more than your company is currently spending. But "constant" research is becoming a fact of organizational life. If you doubt it, just go into a supermarket with an electronic grocery cart, one that records how much time you spend shopping for produce, how much time for cereal, and so on. Information is power, and there's more of it than ever before. We need to harness that power through research. Before the end of this century, most organizations will allocate an astonishing 25% of their budgets to research. It's inevitable, and many futuristic corporations are already moving in that direction.

KEEPING YOUR FOCUS

Maintaining a consistent, resolute focus on the customers' superior need is difficult for any organization.

Literally hundreds of distractions—from financial problems to mergers to foreign competition—can push customers into the background. We've had clients who were phenomenally successful at responding to customer needs. But then a few years passed, and they're at our door again asking for our help in pinpointing a new need that somehow escaped their notice.

It happens, and there's no way to guarantee that you'll always be on top of your customers' needs. But here are a few tactics to shift the odds in your favor.

1. **Keep the number of relationships your organization attempts to maintain in balance with the number of relationships you can effectively manage.**

Though it's tough for many corporations to accept, they can no longer be all things to all people. Too many companies are trying to serve too many markets. They've spread themselves thin, and they simply can't keep track of all their different customer relationships—they lack the resources to do so.

The solution is to become smaller—to move toward a smaller, more sustainable customer base. As humbling as it might be, you can only maintain good customer relationships with a finite group—you may have to sell off some businesses and retreat from some markets to reach that finite number.

2. **Automate as fast as you can.**

The motive here is building better customer relationships, not better-looking bottom lines. We need to reorganize the people who work for our organizations, shifting them away from tasks that could be more efficiently handled by a machine and toward customer relationship building. An organization's resources are limited, and they usually can't spare the people necessary to monitor the customer's voice on a regular basis.

Therefore, seize every technological innovation of value that comes down the pike, verify that it will work for you, implement it and then retrain and shift people into customer relationship positions.

3. **Find someone inside or outside of your company who can do strategic market research.**

In your search for superior customer needs, you're going to need to use a variety of research people. Whether they're inside or outside your organization, choose them for their ability to do strategic research. Traditional researchers don't care how you incorporate and use the data they feed you. On the opposite end of the spectrum, traditional strategists offer ivory tower pronouncements that are divorced from customer need data—they tell you a big trend is coming based on their "years of experience in observing and analyzing the industry." Neither of these types will get you where you want to go. Pure data or pure speculation won't work.

A strategic market researcher, on the other hand, bases projections and analysis on extensive interviews with customers. There should be a solid basis for what you are told, and the researcher should be accountable for his recommendations. He should be willing to form a relationship with you that is tied to the success (or lack thereof) of the strategic analysis that will be provided to you.

CUSTOMER SATISFACTION AND QUALITY ARE JUST STARTING POINTS

There's nothing wrong (and there's a lot right) with customer satisfaction theories and total quality management methods. But they will only take you so far. They're based on old standards. It used to be sufficient to satisfy your customers. Now you have to delight them.

I've used a variety of words and phrases to describe the process of delighting customers: *superior need, hyperservice, partnership fervor.* All these words suggest ways to go beyond the norm in customer relationships; all suggest methods of raising the standards.

It's time to think of the customer in more than superficial terms. I firmly believe that despite all the closed-ended research corporations conduct, they know relatively little about the people they serve. I'm convinced that many organizations are content to meet the existing customer need rather than the emerging one. I've observed companies that fail to factor in what their customers really want in their strategic planning.

I've also seen companies that truly delight their customers. They have a keen eye for their customers' superior need. They are companies where every time their quality team wants to move forward, someone holds up his hand and queries, "Did we ask the customer?" And even if the answer is yes, someone asks a follow-up question: "In the context of what—what type of customer, what environment was he referring to, what definition did he give us?" These organizations probe their customers' answers until they're reasonably certain they have an accurate response.

Each manager in these organizations frequently stops and examines the tasks that make up his and his subordinates' day and asks a very simple question: "What do all these things have to do with what the customer really wants?" Anything that has nothing to do with the customer quickly is disposed of. No matter who originated the idea or how brilliant it might be, it's eliminated because it has nothing to do with meeting a critical customer need.

Throughout this book, I've preached what I practice. Each day, my consulting firm wrestles with superior need issues related to product quality, customer service, emergencies, delivery, price, research and development, and image. Each day, we listen long and hard for the customer voice. Each day, we attempt to help our clients understand what that voice is saying and how they can develop strategies to meet their business goals.

More so than most, we've been successful in enabling our clients to reach their objectives. What works for them should work for you. Try it and see if your customers respond with delight, not just once, but over and over again.

INDEX

About the Publisher

PROBUS PUBLISHING COMPANY

Probus Publishing Company fills the informational needs of today's business professional by publishing authoritative, quality books on timely and relevant topics, including:

- Investing
- Futures/Options Trading
- Banking
- Finance
- Marketing and Sales
- Manufacturing and Project Management
- Personal Finance, Real Estate, Insurance and Estate Planning
- Entrepreneurship
- Management

Probus books are available at quantity discounts when purchased for business, educational or sales promotional use. For more information, please call the Director, Corporate/Institutional Sales at 1-800-PROBUS-1, or write:

Director, Corporate/Institutional Sales
Probus Publishing Company
1925 N. Clybourn Avenue
Chicago, Illinois 60614
FAX (312) 868-6250